The
Motivation
Toolkit

DAVID M. KREPS

The Motivation Toolkit

HOW TO ALIGN YOUR EMPLOYEES' INTERESTS WITH YOUR OWN

W. W. NORTON & COMPANY

Independent Publishers Since 1923

NEW YORK   LONDON

Names and identifying details of some companies and events portrayed in this book have been changed.

For information about permission to reproduce selections from this book, write to Permissions, W. W. Norton & Company, Inc., 500 Fifth Avenue, New York, NY 10110

For information about special discounts for bulk purchases, please contact W. W. Norton Special Sales at specialsales@wwnorton.com or 800-233-4830

Manufacturing by LSC Harrisonburg
Book design by Ellen Cipriano
Production manager: Julia Druskin

ISBN: 978-0-393-25409-9

W. W. Norton & Company, Inc., 500 Fifth Avenue, New York, N.Y. 10110
www.wwnorton.com

W. W. Norton & Company Ltd., 15 Carlisle Street, London W1D 3BS

1 2 3 4 5 6 7 8 9 0

CONTENTS

ACKNOWLEDGMENTS

would like to acknowledge and thank a number of people, both groups and individuals, for their contributions to this book.

James Baron is first and foremost. It would not be at all inaccurate to describe this book as the "*Classics Illustrated*" version of the textbook, *Strategic Human Resources: Frameworks for General Managers*, that I wrote with Jim. People are complex animals, so managing them is complex, and if the reader finds the content of this book to be of interest and of use, I cannot too strongly recommend the longer, more detailed, and more nuanced textbook. But, beyond this, Jim taught me a lot of whatever wisdom this book contains, and I'm grateful to him for that and for our friendship.

Other colleagues, both economists but especially members of Stanford Graduate School of Business (Stanford GSB) faculty who are not economists, have been generous with their time and insights as I put this book together. In alphabetical order, I am grateful in particular to Jennifer Aaker, William Barnett, Glenn Carroll, Francis Flynn, Robert Gibbons, Deborah Gruenfeld,

Michael Hannan, Tamar Kreps, David Larcker, Edward Lazear, Neil Malhotra, James March, William Meehan, Dale Miller, Benoit Monin, Charles O'Reilly, Paul Oyer, Jeffrey Pfeffer, Hayagreeva Rao, Peter Reiss, Kathryn Shaw, Jesper Sorensen, Larissa Tiedens, and Mark Wolfson. (I apologize for any inadvertent omissions.)

This book is, of course, about management, and I learned a lot about management in general, managing human resources, and motivation, by working for and with a master of these crafts, Robert Joss.

Generations of MBA students and Stanford Executive Program participants learned this material along with me and, in so doing, taught me a lot.

Many people at W. W. Norton contributed to the construction of this book, perhaps too many to cite by name. But, in particular, Jeff Shreve picked up this project in midstream and made many important contributions to the organization and exposition of the book. And when Jeff left Norton near the completion of the book, Brendan Curry and Nathaniel Dennett, together with production manager Julia Druskin, did an excellent job in shepherding the book to the end.

Finally, I was encouraged to begin and, every step along the way, to continue working on this book by Jack Repcheck, who previously had edited two textbooks on economics that I wrote. Jack's untimely death prevented him from seeing this book to completion, but both as friend and editor, his "imprint" is found everywhere within these pages. It is with profound sadness for his passing but with wonderful memories of him that I dedicate this book to his memory.

The Motivation Toolkit

Mastering Employee Motivation

This book addresses the question, *How should an organization—* whether a for-profit start-up, a large corporation, or a not-for-profit—*motivate the people who work for it, to get the best possible results?* Getting motivational practices right is certainly not the only thing you must do to be successful as a manager. But it is crucial to achieving success.

Motivating employees is simultaneously becoming more difficult and more important, as economic activity shifts from the so-called old economy to the new. In a larger and larger share of the economy, organizations need employees who work with their heads as well as their hands, who think and act creatively, whose job involves self-starting and self-monitoring. Monitoring employees to ensure that they do a specific and well-defined task is often infeasible or, when feasible, terribly expensive. And it is often ineffective. Rewarding employees piece-rate style—trying to motivate them to perform that specific task more often and more quickly—works well in some cases. But pay for performance fails dramatically in other cases. When it isn't clear a priori what employees ought to be doing, when creativity and proaction are desirable, and when employees are expected to allocate their time among several tasks in response to information they see and the employer does not, then motivating employees to do the right thing is difficult and, at the same time, hugely important to organizational success.

And, in many cases, motivation isn't a matter of you (the employer) actively motivating your employees. Instead, you motivate employees most effectively by eliminating *demotivating* factors.

You can find all sorts of simple answers to the question, *How should you motivate employees?* A Google search of the phrase *motivating employees* yields 17 million results.* Lots of management gurus know the answer and are happy to share with you what they know. Unhappily, if you read through a selection of these answers, you probably come away more confused than when you began, because what one guru knows to be true, another knows is simple nonsense.

The problem is that there is no single best answer to the question. The best answer for you, in your specific situation, will depend on all sorts of factors that bear on your specific situation. Indeed, it can be a bad idea to look for *the best answer*, because motivation is but one of a larger set of human resource management (HRM) issues, all of which tie together in complex ways. The very best way to motivate your employees may have adverse and unanticipated consequences on other HRM issues, such as

---

* At least, it did so on October 26, 2016.

recruitment, or training, or striking the right balance between insourcing and outsourcing. What you should look for instead is *a really good answer* or, if the potential effects of your motivational strategy on other aspects of HRM are severe enough, a *good-enough* answer.

To give you a taste of the complexities of motivation and an example of such unanticipated consequences, consider the following parable drawn from real life. (In this story, and in the story of Zephyr Corporation and their employees in Chapter 4, I construct fictitious examples that are composites of real-life cases, with invented names and details. All other examples, concerning named real-life organizations, are based on publicly available information, although in the simple calculations I do in Chapter 2 concerning Safelite, I invent numbers to simplify the exposition.)

The Sad Story of Artisans' Alliance

The Artisans' Alliance (AA) was formed by a visionary and socially minded group of entrepreneurs, who wished to help third-world artisans bring their merchandise to first-world markets. The business plan was simple: AA employed young men and women to go into underdeveloped countries, looking for artisans and craftspeople of exceptional skill and talent. When such an artisan was "discovered," the employee of AA would offer a partnership, providing technical assistance in arranging to export the artisan's wares to first-world countries, where AA would act as intermediary in placing the wares in small, high-end retail stores. The young men and women who traveled the globe—called *Explorers* by AA—were expected to provide to their client-artisans assistance in logistics and in growing their local shops to the extent feasible while maintaining quality. The Explorers were the key to the operation. Their consummate effort in locating and then supporting exceptional artisans, while building close personal relations with "their" artisans, provided AA with an expanding supply of outstanding goods. Successful Explorers had very marketable language and interpersonal skills. AA paid Explorers less than they could have made working for larger organizations but, for the most part, the Explorers stuck with AA and provided truly outstanding effort.

How was this accomplished? What motivated the Explorers? The simple answer was the mission. The Explorers were idealistic individuals who believed that AA was bringing resources and development to the third world, something very worthwhile to be doing, even if it meant a level of personal sacrifice.

But then AA hit a significant bump in the road. The company was approached by several giant retailers who asked to be clients. Top management at AA saw this as a great—but dangerous—opportunity to scale their business. They worried that giant retailers would take advantage of them, pushing for lower prices and more goods of lower quality. Top management didn't feel that they had the skills required to deal effectively with the giant retailers, and so they went out to hire the expertise they lacked.

The people they approached came from a sales culture very different from that of AA. The best of their prospective new employees expected high base salaries, lavish expense accounts, and commissions on the sales they made. Top management at AA gulped hard at these demands but acquiesced; better to have the sharks working for them than to wind up as shark food.

But, then, their troubles began. The new sales reps were sent out "into the field" to meet with the Explorers, to get a sense of the unique backstories that went with the goods the Explorers had located. And the Explorers were aghast upon meeting these new employees of AA: They were aghast at their lavish (expense-account-fueled) spending and, even more, at the sales reps' prospects for compensation that far exceeded anything any Explorer was paid. Of course, the Explorers still had their cherished mission. But the mission seemed somewhat tarnished by top management's decision to hire these mercenary sales reps. The Explorers wondered why they weren't getting similar personal rewards. The notion was hatched that maybe top managers were exploiting the Explorers' good and generous nature for their own private ends. Turnover among Explorers spiked upward, and when the small HR department at AA surveyed the Explorers' job satisfaction, they found a strong positive correlation between dissatisfaction and the amount of time Explorers had spent with the new sales reps.

AA had a great mission-based motivational scheme working for its key in-the-field employees, the Explorers. And, when they went to hire a new class of employees, they motivated the new employees by what may well have been the best possible scheme for those new employees. But in doing so, they turned extremely well motivated Explorers into disgruntled and less well motivated employees.

The point of the story is simple: Motivation within an organization is complex. It is not a matter of looking at a single employee or one class of employees and answering the question, *What's the best way to motivate this (or these) employees?* To get motivation right, you must think broadly, and to think broadly, you need tools for organizing your thoughts. Could AA have done better? How could they have done better? I'll give you my suggestions later in this book, after we have developed those tools.

My Focus: Type-K Employees and Consummate Performance

Employees and the work they do come in a variety of types. Some employees perform very specific and set functions. Others, such as the Explorers of Artisans' Alliance, have jobs in which they must exercise substantial discretion concerning what they do and how they do it, jobs that call for outside-the-box thinking, creativity, and cooperation with other employees, and whose on-the-job quality of performance is difficult to measure, at least in the short run. Phrases that you may hear describing such employees and their jobs are "working with their heads and not just their hands," or "knowledge workers." I'll use the phrase *Type-K* (as in "knowledge") *jobs* for jobs with some or all of these characteristics.

My focus is on motivating employees in Type-K jobs. Moreover, my focus is on motivating them to provide *consummate performance*, going above and beyond any nominal job description or specification, doing the very best job (for the organization) that is possible as opposed to doing what is "required" and no more, which I'll call *perfunctory performance*.

Characteristics of Type-K jobs

- The employee with this job must attend to several different tasks and must allocate his or her time among them.
- The tasks to be done are, *ex ante*, ambiguous. What to do next involves the results of work done so far and the resolution of environmental uncertainty, in ways that neither the employee nor supervisors can anticipate initially.
- The tasks involve creativity by the employee or, at least, thinking and then acting "outside the box" on occasion.
- Outcomes are hard to describe, let alone measure, in the short run.
- Insofar as outcomes can be measured, they are the result of the efforts of multiple employees.
- Cooperation among employees is important to the organization.
- The technology is such that the employee has substantial effective autonomy, making on-the-job choices with little supervision or guidance from supervisors.

Motivation = Alignment

The traditional image of the relationship between a supervisor and subordinate (or employer and employee) is that the boss tells her subordinates what to do and what not to do, and monitors their compliance with these dos and don'ts, with dire consequences in case of violations.

With Type-K jobs, this method of "control" is not going to work well. If you, the boss, can't say up front what your employees should do beyond "be creative" or "cooperate," and if you can't tell after the fact how well or how hard they tried to fulfill your commands, dos and don'ts alone probably won't buy you more than perfunctory performance.

And, in fact, dos and don'ts often provoke behavior that you *don't* want. People tend to resent limitations or rules imposed on them and actively attempt to subvert such limitations and rules. A classic dramatic storyline involves a new resident in a dark and creepy Victorian mansion who is told, "Whatever you do, you must not go into that room." This, we all know, means that the individual will go into that room, with unpleasant consequences. This might be blamed on curiosity; in the work context, it is probably more often the psychological "discomfort" that comes from feeling controlled, which is best mitigated by the employee showing his or her ability to control their own actions by going against what they are told to do and not do. Psychologists call this phenomenon *reactance*.

You, as employer, might think that with cleverly designed rules and restrictions, you can frustrate the employee's innate desire to circumvent them. And there is a sense in which this is so: Psychological research suggests that reactance is strongest when the individual is most conscious of the rules and restrictions that are imposed. If you can design the desired rules and restrictions in ways that don't engage the employee's active cognitive processes, you will in this regard be better off. But this is a tall order. Posing the rules as "guidelines" may dull reactance, because it gives the employee the sense that he has some measure of control. But if rules are merely dressed up as "guidelines," employees will see through the window dressing. Finally, designing rules and restrictions that take a lot of employee creativity and guile to circumvent may seem a good idea. But clever control mechanisms are apt to engender equally clever attempts to subvert the control. This is not how you want your employees using their creative energies.

So what is the alternative to direct control; that is, to dos and don'ts? Robert M. Bass, one of the most successful and distinguished graduates of Stanford GSB, summarized his HRM strategy as follows:

> I have developed three inviolate principles that I apply to my business:
>
> 1. Find people of great skill, integrity, creativity, and judgment.
>
> 2. Put them in positions where the wind is at their backs.
>
> 3. Design a structure that aligns their interests closely with mine, support them when they ask for help, but otherwise empower them to do what they do best.[1]

This is so well said that it probably doesn't need a paraphrase, but I want to hammer home this point, so: First, employ people with the skill set (and personal values) required for your Type-K job. Second, put them in a situation where they can exercise those skills; don't frustrate a talented employee with finger exercises. And then, third, let them do their thing, *after you have motivated them to make choices that are good for you (as well as for them), by aligning their interests with yours.*

This book is about the third step. Motivation—I should say, effective motivation—is the alignment of your employees' interests with your own. Once that is done (if you have able employees and you give them the opportunity to use their abilities), you stand back and let them use their judgment, creativity, and energy as they see fit.

Restrictions and rules have their place. Sometimes they are the best way to control employees. But they are, in my estimation, employed too often and too quickly, perhaps because they seem the simplest way to get the behavior that the employer desires. Aligning the employee's interests with those of the employer usually seems harder to achieve. But the results are, in my experience, better—increasingly so the more you are dealing with Type-K employees from whom you want consummate performance— when you take the harder route.

And if motivation = alignment, the obvious question is, *How do you align interests?* What tools can you use, what are common pitfalls that arise in their use, and how do you choose among available tools?

My Objective: To Give You Tools

This book does not provide answers to those questions designed to fit your organization. To reiterate from the start of this chapter, no universal answer to *How should you motivate your employees?* exists. I don't know the particulars of your situation, and I firmly believe that those particulars are crucial to effective motivation of your employees.

Instead, my objective is to give you tools that, when applied to your specific situation, will lead you to more effective motivation.

In the final chapter, I provide a list of questions that I would ask you were I to consult with you about how to improve the motivation of your employees. If you answer those questions honestly (and, to give fair warning, some of them will require that you ask your employees about their perceptions), and if you view the answers through the lens of the tools provided in the rest of the book, you won't need me or any other consultant.

The nature of the "tools" is worth describing at the outset: They are frameworks developed by social scientists of several disciplines, most prominently the disciplines of economics and social psychology, with a smidgen of organizational sociology added to the mix. These tools (or frameworks) live on two different levels.

At a more basic level—the foundation, if you will—are frameworks for understanding the employment relationship, both from an economic and from a psychological perspective. Motivation is ultimately about changing the nature of your relationship with your employees, hoping to influence them to behave in ways that you desire. And how your employees behave takes us to the core of their relationship with you, with their work, and with their jobs: what they take from the relationship and what they are willing and able to give in return.

The second level of framework involves motivation specifically. Building from the basic economics and social psychology of employment relationships, we compare and contrast different theories drawn from those disciplines that address motivation, such as the economic theory of incentives and the social-psychological theory of self-determination.

Sometimes these frameworks and theories are complementary. Sometimes they give conflicting prescriptions, because of the differences in the behavioral assumptions on which they are built. It will be up to you to pick and choose among them, based on your intuition, informed by your experiences and your particular answers to questions that the frameworks present.

To be clear: Superficial understanding of the frameworks is insufficient. This book is informed by and tries to communicate ideas that are sometimes subtle and always challenging. At times, you may feel like the book is taking you "back to school." You'll feel that way because taking you back to school—to rethink and reconceptualize the relationship you have with your employees—is exactly what this book is about. I assert that you'll be in a lot better position to figure out how to motivate your employees if you persevere. But at least some perseverance is required.

Two Notes on Style

There's an old-fashioned literary style in which the author addresses remarks directly to the reader, often using the formulation "Dear Reader." I'm not going to go so far as to address you as "Dear Reader," but the literary style of this book is conversational and, specifically, it will seem at times that I'm having a conversation with the head of an organization who is concerned with motivating his or her employees. You—the reader—may not be in that position, just yet. You may not have aspirations of reaching such a position. Even if you don't head your organization or have aspirations to do so someday, if you are in a position where motivating subordinates is part of what you do, I believe that the ideas delivered here will be useful do you. Indeed, even if you are the subordinate, these ideas may help you in dealing with the folks whose job it is to motivate you. But so that the narrative proceeds smoothly, in what follows, "You" will often refer to a CEO, COO, managing partner, division head, or similar. If that isn't you, please imagine yourself in that role.

Also, the use of third-person pronouns these days leads to several unpalatable choices: Do you use he, him, and his; she, her, and hers; he or she, him or her, his or hers; or try to write so that you finesse the issue with they, them, and theirs? When describing specific situations in which a job is largely held by members of one gender or the other, I'll use the historically appropriate pronouns. Therefore, technicians at Safelite Glass will be he, nurses at Beth Israel Hospital in Boston will be she. Otherwise, in cases where there are supervisors and subordinates, she will supervise him. And, in other cases, I'll drift between the two; I hope no confusion will result, and I apologize to anyone who is offended.

Pay for Performance: The Economic Theory of Incentives

If Motivation = Alignment, how do you align the interests of your employees with your own? Economists by and large think they have the right tool for this job: pay for performance, which has the fancy name *incentive theory*. We'll begin there, with a case in which pay for performance led to a big win for the company that employed it.

Safelite Glass[1] is the largest automobile-glass replacement company in the United States. Imagine that something causes your windshield to shatter or develop a crack. Perhaps you call a glass repair and replacement shop directly; more often (in the United States), you call your insurance agent, who then contacts a glass repair and replacement shop. And, in the United States, the second call most often goes to Safelite. After getting the details (make and model of car, extent of damage, location of the vehicle), Safelite dispatches a panel truck or van, loaded with the appropriate tools and replacement glass if needed, driven to the vehicle's location by the *technician*, who does whatever is needed on the spot: cleans up any broken glass, removes the old windshield, and installs a new windshield; or, if the crack is small enough, applies a resin that "clarifies" and strengthens the glass. Safelite will also (as needed) replace side and back windows and mirrors.

Safelite has a variety of employees: management, of course; dispatchers and clericals who handle calls and paperwork and initiate a repair-or-replacement sequence; and warehouse workers, who load the panel trucks and vans. But the key to the operation is the *technician*; the person who drives the loaded truck to the stricken vehicle and does whatever is needed. And who, importantly, does all this on his own. (Technicians are, at the time of this story, still nearly all men, so I'll use *he*, *his*, and *him* for them.)

Nowadays, with the possibility of GPS tracking, serious monitoring of even remotely located technicians is to some extent possible. But, not so long ago, a technician who left the warehouse with a loaded truck could take his time to get to the location of the vehicle, make the repair, and get back. Safelite paid technicians an hourly wage and, to no one's surprise, they found that their technicians took a lot of time to complete each job, more time than management at Safelite thought was necessary or reasonable.

So, Safelite decided to try to motivate its technicians—to align the interests of technicians with those of Safelite—with a modified piece-rate system it called PPP. A piece rate was set for each type of job, and a technician would be paid each week the sum of the piece-rate payments he had earned, subject to one modification: Safelite backstopped the technicians' wages with a guaranteed minimum hourly wage: If the sum of the piece-rate payments earned in a given week fell below what the technician would be paid according to this guaranteed hourly wage, the technician would be paid by the hour, at least as long as the technician achieved a minimum (acceptable) amount of work in his time on the job. (This minimum was, roughly, what technicians had been accomplishing before PPP.)

To implement PPP, Safelite had to set a number of parameters, including, of course, the piece rate for each type of job. But, in addition, Safelite's management had to decide on the guaranteed minimum wage rate. Two opinions emerged about what minimum wage rate to set. Some members of top management argued that the guarantee should be less than the currently paid hourly wage; it should be 70% of what technicians earned before the new system was put in place. "If," they argued, "the guarantee is set (say) at the current wage rate, then no technician would make less under the new system than previously, and our labor bill can only increase."

But another group favored setting the minimum at 100% of the current wage rate, pointing out that even if this was done, Safelite's bottom line could still be improved. First, if the new system motivates technicians to work more quickly, customers would become more satisfied—sitting on a roadside waiting for your vehicle to be repaired is not fun—which might mean more business for Safelite.

Second, and perhaps more significantly, if the piece rates are set at levels below former unit labor costs, then any technician who does enough to get into the piece-rate region will be working more efficiently; for the same volume of total work, Safelite can employ fewer technicians, and so its total wage bill (for the same volume of work) declines, even if the technicians who remain are paid more.

Let me flesh out the second point with a caricature. Suppose that, previously, technicians were paid $12 per hour for a 40-hour workweek, giving gross pay of $480 per week. Suppose (here is the caricature part) the only task done by technicians is to replace windshields, and technicians by and large have managed to do 10 windshields per week. Unit labor cost (per windshield replaced) is then $48 per windshield. If Safelite's national "load" is 5,000 windshields per week, and if technicians do (on average) 10 windshields a week, Safelite needs to employ 500 technicians, for a weekly technician wage bill of 500 × $480 = $240,000 (plus taxes and benefits, which I'll ignore) per week.

Suppose that Safelite sets the piece rate of a windshield job at $30 per windshield. Some technicians may choose to work harder, to earn more; note that at a piece rate of $30 per windshield, a technician must finish more than 16 windshields in a week to make more than the $480 guaranteed wage rate. Suppose that 100 of the technicians do 20 windshields a week, earning $600 each week; the rest are unwilling to work this hard, and continue to average 10 windshields each, taking their guarantee of $480. The point is that, of the 5,000 windshields that must be done, the 100 hardworking technicians do 2,000, leaving only 3,000 for the lazier technicians. And at 10 windshields each week, this means Safelite needs only 300 of the lazier technicians. Once Safelite is able to reduce its technician workforce to the new required level of 400, the wage bill is 100 × $600 + 300 × $480 = $204,000 per week, 85% of what it was before. There is no magic here: If part of the workforce has an average unit labor cost of $48 per windshield, while the rest averages $30 per windshield, the overall average is going to go down from when everyone averaged $48 per windshield. It may take a while for Safelite to get the number of technicians it employs down to the new required level, so this doesn't mean instantly increased profit. But, in the longer run, this is the effect.

Of course, this does *not* imply that a guarantee of 100% of former wage rates is best for Safelite. They might do even better if they cut the guarantee to, say, 70% of the previous guarantee. But it does show that Safelite could keep the guarantee at 100% of the old wage rate and, after adjusting its workforce levels, improve its bottom line.

The Fundamental Idea of Rewards for Performance

What's going on here? The fundamental idea of piece-rate systems is that employees like more money in their pocket and, *at least in some cases*, are willing to work harder for it. An employer can try to make sure employees are all working hard with a combination of monitoring and exhortation; or the employer can provide employees with the incentive to work harder, letting the employee *choose* how hard to work. Put in the language of Chapter 1, it is in the interests of Safelite for technicians to complete more work per week, so that Safelite can employ fewer technicians. By rewarding technicians who are willing to work faster, Safelite aligns the interests of those technicians with the interests of Safelite. The alignment isn't perfect, of course, but it is a step in the right direction.

And note well: A nice feature of letting the employee choose is that this system simultaneously accommodates a variety of workers. Each employee is offered the same menu of pay-for-performance options; those employees who are content with lower effort and lower pay are free to make that choice, while those who are willing to work harder to earn more have that option, leading to higher overall satisfaction.

The same fundamental idea is at work in other pay-for-performance schemes. Employees are rewarded—with bigger raises or bonus payments—the more that they make choices at work that benefit the organization. The employee is somewhat free to choose what she wants, but a well-constructed pay-for-performance scheme motivates her to make choices that are good both for herself and for her employer. Indeed, *pay* for performance is too restrictive a formulation of this idea: Think in terms of *rewards* for performance, where the rewards can be anything the employee values: more money in the pay packet, of course, but also praise, promotion, autonomy, and so forth.

The Fundamental Problem with Rewards for Performance

But this fundamental idea immediately runs up against an equally fundamental problem. Everything works like a charm if the employer can observe what choices the employee makes. Unhappily, in most cases, the employer instead observes measures of *output* that are determined *only in part* by what the employee chooses to do; output also depends to some extent on factors that the employee does not control. If the rewards provided the employee depend on those measures of output, the employee's compensation is risky from his perspective, and many employees are averse to risk in how much money they take home at the end of the week.

For instance, at the start of a given week, an ambitious Safe-lite technician thinks, "I'm going to work hard this week and do 20 windshields, so at the end of the week I'll be rewarded with $600." But what if this technician does put in a high level of effort and, for reasons outside his control—I'll give a list of such reasons later—only manages to do 12 windshields, earning $360? Of course, the technician could have had good luck concerning those factors he doesn't control and completed 25 windshields, earning $750. But, the point is, since his compensation depends directly on the number of windshields he completes, which is only indirectly connected to how much effort he puts in, he faces (for a fixed level of effort) a random level of income. And, to the extent that he is risk averse—that is, he doesn't appreciate this uncertainty in his weekly pay, because he has mortgage and car payments to make, or because he lives from paycheck to paycheck—this makes him wary of the whole scheme.

The juxtaposition of the fundamental idea with this fundamental problem is the starting point for the *economic theory of incentives*, which at its most basic level is about balancing incentives for the employee and providing the employee with "insurance" against the things he cannot control.

The Wage Guarantee at Safelite

Which level of wage guarantee is best for Safelite? The answer to this question involves a number of considerations:

1. Turnover of technicians is a sizeable expense for Safelite. In this business, some level of turnover—in fact, a significant level of turnover—is inevitable; the pool of prospective employees for this sort of semiskilled labor consists in part of people who move from job to job (or, from job to spells of unemployment) frequently. So one consideration is: What will be the impact on Safelite's turnover rates of the different guarantees? Advocates for the 100% guarantee were particularly concerned about turnover in the short run. A new compensation system that offered a guarantee less than what the technicians were previously making would anger some of the currently employed technicians, who might then quit in droves.

2. But advocates for cutting the guarantee felt that, if Safelite cut the guarantee, more technicians would choose to put in enough effort to be on the piece-rate part of the compensation scheme. With a 100% guarantee, a technician's choice is to do 10 windshields per week and earn $480, or do 17 or more (at the $30 piece rate) to earn more. But with a 70% guarantee, which is $336 per week, the same technician only needs to increase his work rate by 20% (to 12 per week) to beat the guarantee.

And even if a technician is so work-averse as to settle for 10 windshields and $336, this gives a unit labor cost of $33.60 for Safelite, instead of $48 per windshield with the 100% guarantee. Bottom line: With the lower guarantee, more technicians will opt for doing more than the minimum, at a unit cost of $30, and those who don't choose to do more than 10 still provide those 10 at lower cost per unit.

3. Moreover, advocates for a lower guarantee argued that turnover of technicians who would be angered by the new system was not a bad thing, in the longer run. A technician willing to work hard enough to be above the guarantee—a low-unit-labor-cost technician, in other words—wouldn't care about the guarantee, so wouldn't be angry and wouldn't leave. It is the high-unit-labor-cost technicians, those who would not exert themselves, who would be angry and leave: Safelite would be shedding technicians who, in the longer run, it didn't want anyway. And it would be attractive as an employer *mostly* to technicians who were willing to work hard. In the longer run, the quality of its workforce—measured in terms of the proportion of employees willing to work hard—would improve.

4. But the advocates for the 100% guarantee brought up the fundamental complication: To reiterate, a technician might *want* to work hard and do more than 16 windshields in a week, therefore earning at least his

old weekly wage of $480, but he can't *guarantee* this outcome, no matter how hard he tries. Even a super-ambitious and hardworking technician might be assigned jobs far from his home base, so that driving to and from the jobs would take a lot of time. The weather might slow him down. He might be given the wrong-size windshield by the warehouse operators, requiring two trips to the job. He might be ill for part of the week. And there might simply be a dearth of jobs to do, leaving him sitting idly at his home base, waiting for work to come in. The net of all this is that the super-ambitious, hardworking technician faces uncertainty in how much he can make in a week. The guarantee, for this technician, is his insurance policy against a week in which his level of jobs completed is below normal. And, assuming he lives week-to-week on his paycheck (pretty typical for these employees), with monthly rent and car payments to make, that insurance is important to him. A backstop weekly paycheck of $480 is a much better insurance policy than, say, a backstop of $336. But, on the other hand, a bigger guarantee weakens the techni-cian's incentives to exert himself, which takes us back to point 2.

The Fundamental Trade-off in Incentive Theory

This example illustrates the fundamental trade-off in the eco-nomic theory of incentives. You wish to motivate an employee to work harder, smarter, or both. You can take a "stick" approach and monitor the employee carefully and continuously, with the (implicit or explicit) threat that an employee caught slacking off will be fired. Or, instead, and especially if monitoring carefully and continuously is too costly or impossible (as was the case with Safelite technicians), you can adopt a "carrot" approach: Provide greater compensation the harder or smarter the employee works, thereby aligning the employee's interests with those of the organization and motivating the desired behavior, at least among those employees for whom the work-better-and-get-more-compensation trade-off is worthwhile.

But in many cases, it is hard to measure directly how hard-working or smart an employee is, so incentive compensation is based instead on observable measures of "outcome" that, in a statistical fashion, correlate with the desired behavior.

For instance, although a firm that employs salespersons who make sales calls cannot monitor the effort the salesperson puts into each call, it can measure how many sales the salesperson makes. And a salesperson knows that putting in more effort is likely to generate more sales. So compensating the salesperson with a base salary plus a percentage commission for each sale made should motivate the salesperson to put in more effort.

But more effort by the salesperson doesn't guarantee more sales. No matter how hard the salesperson tries with a particular prospect, some prospective customers will not buy. And, even if she sells to all her prospects, some prospects take more time and effort than others, decreasing the number of prospects she can reach. Hence, a salesperson on commission has an uncertain level of income, a level that is partially in her control—influenced by how hard she works—but partially not. Now, *in theory*, if the salesperson didn't mind risks—if she valued every risky prospect at its expected or average value—the optimal thing to do is to give the salesperson 100% of the profits generated by her sales and have her pay the employer for the opportunity to make sales and thereby earn this income.* But the stakes are often enormous. Think, for instance, of someone trying to sell a business-services contract for which the profit to the firm providing the services will be $5 million if the sale is made. Suppose the chance of the sale being made, if the salesperson puts in a lot of effort, is 50%. A salesperson who doesn't care about risks and whose bank account is very, very healthy might be willing to *pay* the company for which she works their expected profit of $2.5 million less some amount for her time and effort, if in return she is paid $5 million if she makes the sale. But very few salespersons have the working capital, and disregard for huge risk, needed to take such a gamble.

Salespeople and other employees do care about risk, in most cases. So, to shield the salesperson from risks in her compensation, the company offers a base wage together with a commission rate less than 100%. To increase the effectiveness of this shield—to increase the amount of "insurance" given the salesperson—the company should lower the commission rate while increasing the base salary. But while this enhances the protection against risk, it simultaneously lowers the salesperson's incentive to work hard. Or, put the other way, the company can increase the incentive facing the salesperson by increasing the commission rate and decreas-

---

* At least, that's what comes out of an economic-theory analysis of this situation. You'll need to consult a good economics textbook—one that provides formal models of incentive theory—to see why.

ing her base salary, which raises the amount of risk she faces. This is the fundamental trade-off in incentive theory: the balance between incentive and insurance. This is not an easy trade-off to get right for a variety of reasons (for instance, it depends on how averse to risks is the employee, which is not something that employers readily know), but it is a trade-off that must be faced in almost every incentive or pay-for-(apparent)-performance scheme.[2]

What did Safelite do concerning this trade-off? In the end, Safelite decided on a 100%-of-previous-wage-rates guarantee. And, even with this high-guarantee level—advocates of the high guarantee might argue, *in part because of* the high guarantee level—the new compensation system was a big win for Safelite. Unit labor costs decreased by around 30%. Empirical analysis suggests that about half the decrease came from "incentive effects," where technicians who had been working slowly were (now) motivated to increase the amount of work they did; the other half came from what economists call "screening effects": The new compensation system made Safelite a more attractive employer to ambitious and hardworking employees, increasing the relative retention rate of ambitious and hardworking types, relative to lazier types, and (especially) increasing the relative intake rate of ambitious types. Therefore, the percentage of technicians who opted for PPP increased as time passed.[3]

Complications and Elaborations

Pay for performance—in the simple form of piece-rate pay or in more elaborate forms—can be an extremely effective tool, as was the case at Safelite. But pay for performance can be dangerous. The most obvious danger is that rewarding "results" can lead to employee actions that are entirely undesirable. In 2016, for example, Wells Fargo Bank made the news when its pay-for-performance scheme went awry. Wells Fargo's marketing strategy involves cross-selling, getting checking-account customers to open credit-card or investment accounts, for instance. So, to align the interests of customer-facing bank employees with this strategy, the bank offered those employees bounties for successful cross-sales. As long as the bank was careful to be sure that those cross-sales were legitimate, this scheme might have worked well. But, to the apparent dismay of top management, employees were enrolling customers in accounts without bothering to get the consent of the customers. As I write these words, it is unclear what the long-term impact will be on the bank. But the fallout caused CEO and chair John Stumpf to step down from both positions. And this is not an isolated incident: It is a tautology to say that incentives do what they are meant to do, they motivate behavior. You had better be sure that the behavior motivated is what is desired.

But, beyond such obvious incentives-induced malfeasance, pay for performance raises a number of issues—complications and elaborations on the basic theory—that require careful attention. These complications and elaborations are of increasing importance the more complex is the job being done. But, even at Safe-lite, the system raised issues that required attention. Here are some of the most important of these complications and elaborations:

Eliminating (or, at Least, Ameliorating) Extraneous Risk

The fundamental trade-off arises because the outcomes on which the employee's rewards are based don't perfectly reflect how much or what sort of effort she supplied. Economists describe this sort of situation by saying that outcomes are a "noisy" signal of efforts. It stands to reason that less "noise" will mean more effec-tive incentives and, *according to this theory*, this is usually true. I've emphasized *according to this theory* because it is not the only theory going; see the discussion of stock options at the end of this chap-ter and then in Chapter 6. But, for the time being, assume that less noise means more effective incentives.

Therefore, if you are going to implement this sort of incentive scheme for your employees, you should think very hard about the risks they can't control but, perhaps, you can eliminate or, at least, reduce. For instance, in the case of Safelite:

- One risk factor in how much work a technician can do in a week is the distance he must drive to and from jobs to which he is assigned. Better assignment and dispatch can help ameliorate this, and Safelite invested substan-tially in improving their assignment and dispatch pro-cesses as they implemented PPP.

- Finding, upon arrival at the job site, that the glass loaded on his truck by the warehouse folks is the wrong size or defective, is not pleasant for a technician. So Safelite, as it implemented PPP, invested in improving its warehouse operations.

- If Safelite's glass suppliers had quality-control problems that would result occasionally in new windshields shattering upon installation—I'm unaware whether they had such a problem, so this is a conditional assertion—it would certainly improve matters for the technicians if Safelite took steps to improve the quality of its glass.

And, more generally, in piece-rate contexts where the piece-rate activity is one step in a longer chain of steps from raw materials to finished goods, firms often find that they must increase the amount of work-in-process (WIP) inventory they hold, so that ambitious employees are not starved of work to do.

It is worth noting that an increase of WIP inventory is, by itself, costly to the organization. When Safelite invests in better dispatch, it benefits along with its technicians: Reducing the time technicians spend driving to and from jobs both allows technicians to do more jobs more quickly—so Safelite can make do with fewer technicians—and results in happier customers, who are waiting less for the repair truck to arrive. Improved warehouse operations and higher quality glass are similarly good for both Safelite and its technicians. The point is that, having moved to PPP, the returns to Safelite from investing in better dispatch, better warehouse operations, and better glass, which were positive to begin with, were all enhanced. Before PPP, these improvements were (perhaps) not worthwhile given their cost. But investments in them were justified once PPP was implemented. On the other hand, increasing WIP inventory to enhance a piece-rate implementation runs against the organization's general interests to reduce inventory.

And, in the sort of service-on-demand business in which Safelite is engaged, piece-rate pay can *lower* the returns from otherwise profit-enhancing investments. When, in this sort of business, business arrives somewhat randomly, customer satisfaction is enhanced by having more capacity in service—that is, more technicians—than one needs on average. That way, when there is a sudden surge in calls for service, the company is better able to handle the load quickly. But, with PPP, having more technicians than are typically needed comes at a cost: Technicians will sometimes be starved of work; and an ambitious technician who is starved of work is an unhappy technician. Moreover, in such a situation, ambitious technicians can try to influence dispatchers to give them the next job that comes in, even if it isn't their "turn," and they can conspire with their fellows: "You are settling this week for the guarantee, so I'll slip you a couple of dollars or buy you a beer after work if you let me have the next job assigned to you."

Finding Better Forms of Insurance

And as the employer thinks through the various factors that employees can't control but that affect the outcomes they achieve, the employer should think what form of "insurance" is most effective for dealing with the risk those factors impose. Safelite's guaranteed minimum wage offers insurance, but it is a fairly blunt insurance instrument.

Suppose that, having improved dispatch and warehouse operations, the remaining uncontrollable risk for technicians is work starvation, where the technician is ready and willing to take another job, but no jobs are available. With a weekly wage guarantee, a technician who has been "starved" on Monday and Tuesday may decide that it is no longer worth working hard on the last three days of the week; the odds of earning above the weekly guarantee are too small. If this is the main remaining risk factor, Safelite might pay an hourly wage to technicians while they are "involuntarily idled" rather than offering a guaranteed weekly wage. This scheme, which is probably the most common way to fix the problem of work starvation in piece-rate settings, is not without its own problems in the context of Safelite, especially if the work available is assigned in strategic fashion: A technician who wants to coast for a few days influences the dispatcher to assign work to other technicians, as long as other technicians are available. But, all things considered, it may give a more efficient overall arrangement than a weekly guarantee.

Benchmarking and Tournaments

Suppose you operate a Honda new-car dealership, and you wish to motivate members of your sales force. You could look at number of cars sold and the margin achieved in those sales as measures of how well each salesperson has done. But these measures are noisy reflections of how well a particular salesman has been selling;

for instance, he may have been unlucky in the draw of customers to whom he was assigned. Particular cars may be difficult to sell because of some new model brought out by the competition. And when the local or national economy is doing poorly, consumers may be generally less inclined to buy new cars.

There isn't much one can do to about the luck of the draw when it comes to customers. But the local or national economy for this Honda salesman is the same as for the nearby Toyota dealership. So by *benchmarking* the performance of a Honda salesman against the overall sales of Toyotas, you can eliminate this sort of "noise," at least to some extent. By this I mean, if sales of Toyotas fall off, but a Honda salesman maintains his level of sales and margins, this indicates excellent (relative) performance by the Honda salesman, so his incentive reward should be higher. Or, put a bit more negatively, if you see sales of Toyotas fall off, you should be less inclined to blame a similar fall-off in the performance of your Honda salesman on his lack of sales effort, and his incentive compensation should be adjusted accordingly.

But what if Toyota introduces a new model that sells like hotcakes and, accordingly, depresses the sales of a competing Honda model? A Honda salesman is not responsible for this decline in sales, and benchmarking against Toyota sales *compounds* the "noise." The best benchmark you can find for a specific Honda salesperson is then the performance of other Honda salespersons. They are selling the same vehicles, in the same economy. So maybe you want to benchmark how one of your salespersons does against the performance of Honda salespersons nationwide, or statewide, or even in your own dealership.

Benchmarking the performance of one salesperson in your

dealership against the performance of your other salespersons would seem to eliminate as much noise as possible. But doing this raises potential problems: If you want your salespersons to act as a team, with one salesperson helping another to make a sale, benchmarking each salesperson against the performance of others introduces adverse incentives; why should Salesperson A help B, when sales made by B has a negative impact on A's compensation? This consideration isn't dispositive; the natural inclination that folks have to help one another (what later will be called the *norm of reciprocity*) can overcome this adverse incentive effect. But, especially in cases where cooperation among employees is crucial, you should watch out for it.

When your benchmark for individual performance is the average performance of other employees doing the same task, you should also watch out for peer pressure in reverse; that is, where rate-busters are "encouraged" by their peers to dial down their efforts. In a similar vein, *re*-setting piece rates downward based on enhanced production rates, particularly when the enhanced production rates are due to implementing a piece-rate scheme, rarely works out well for the employer.

One extreme form of benchmarking (which, to some extent, is present whenever you benchmark employees against each other) is called *tournament-style* compensation, where you give a prize to the best performing employee in a group, or to each of the top 5% in terms of individual performance; think of a case where the salesperson with the best record in each six-month period gets a bonus of $5,000 or a vacation trip to Hawaii and the runner-up gets a weekend for two at a local spa. Tournaments, especially in organizations with a culture of competition, can be very effective. But they certainly raise issues when it comes to cooperation among the "contestants."

Interdependence and Team-Based Incentive Schemes

When employee interdependence is very strong, it can be difficult to get good measures of how well any single employee has performed, making individual-based incentives less useful if not impossible. It is common in such circumstances to resort to team-based incentive schemes: Everyone in a work team gets a bonus or some other prize if the team as a whole performs well. I'm sure that, if you have any experience with this sort of team-based compensation, you can anticipate the major difficulty: The larger the team, the greater the risk that one or more members of the team will try to free ride on the efforts of other team members. Control of this sort of free riding is most often accomplished (or, at least, is attempted) through peer pressure within the team. And peer pressure can work wonders in this regard. But this raises some significant questions about team composition: Since peer pressure is typically based on social rewards, do you want to form teams that are socially coherent (or, in other words, less diverse along demographic lines)? Perhaps you want to let teams form themselves. But if you do that, there is likely to be some tendency for the most able to team up, leaving less able folks to form their own teams. How equitable is that?

Team-based compensation, used for incentive purposes—and whether you intend team-based compensation to have incentive implications or not, it will have incentive implications!—can be tricky. We take up this topic in greater depth in Chapter 7.

Dynamics

It is typical for the performance of an employee to be measured periodically, which compounds his efforts over the full time frame of the "review period." For instance, at Safelite, the review period was one workweek. Insofar as the employee has a sense of how well he is doing before the review period is over, you can get some very bad consequences for incentives near the end of the review period.

Suppose, for instance, a Safelite technician starts the week ready and willing to install 20 windshields, which will earn him $600 for the week. But, on Monday, due to no fault of his own, he does only two, with three more on Tuesday and then two on Wednesday. Then at the start of work on Thursday morning, he has seven done. He can't physically reach 20, and even getting to 17 to take advantage of the PPP rate is a formidable task. So, on Thursday morning, he is likely to decide to settle for the $480 guarantee, which only takes three more over the next two days.*

Why does this happen? Because the formula that translates results (number of windshields installed) into compensation has a *flat spot*—a range of outcomes for which compensation stays the same—from 10 windshields installed to 16 (at least, in our model). You lose the effect of incentive pay if an employee, near the end of a review period, is trapped in one of these flat spots.

And, at the other extreme, suppose Safelite, in an attempt

---

* I'm assuming, for simplicity, that each technician *must* do ten windshields a week or be fired. Reality would be more complex; a hardworking technician is likely to be allowed an occasional week where he does less than ten, as long as it doesn't happen too often and he otherwise has a good performance record.

to get employees to move to PPP, offers an extra incentive to get to 17 windshields: If in a week you do 16 or less, you get $480 (as long as you install at least 10), but from 17 on you get $550 plus $30 per additional windshield. Then moving from 16 to 17 is worth $70. Imagine the behavior of a technician who, on Friday morning, is sitting at 15. Or imagine the same technician who gets his 16th assignment at 1 pm on Friday afternoon. I'd hate to be driving on the same roads as this guy, as he speeds to and from job #16, trying to squeeze in job #17 before quitting time. And I'd hate to be the dispatcher, if the technician gets back to the shop at 3:45 on Friday afternoon and puts on whatever pressure he can for one last job. (Though being the dispatcher in this situation might be a good thing, if the norms of the shop are that dispatchers can be bribed for assignments.)

A famous example of this sort of thing, on an organizational rather than an individual scale, involves the glory attached to a car manufacturer who sells (in the United States) the greatest number of a given model in a calendar year. The Honda Accord was the first "foreign" car to win this contest, beginning in 1989 and holding the title in 1990 and 1991. But late in 1992, it was clear that the Ford Taurus was challenging Honda's cherished first-place ranking; late that year, it was a neck-and-neck race. You can imagine the great deals you could get on both Accords and Tauruses in the last two weeks of December that year, as dealers of both brands were given all sorts of special incentives by their manufacturers to get Accords and Tauruses out the door before December 31. (And, if it became clear on December 23 that Ford had taken an insurmountable lead, Honda might "flip" and give its salespersons incentives to put off sales until early in the following calendar year. This isn't hard to do: Cancel special incentives for dealers for the rest of the calendar year, while letting them know that they will get special incentives beginning January 1.)

One employment context in which this sort of thing is seen is in tournament schemes, where there are only a few "winners." Imagine, for instance, a sales organization that gives a special bonus to whoever sells the most in each quarter. And, to build a spirit of competition, the organization posts results daily: A quick check of the company's internal website on any day will tell everyone involved how much each salesperson has sold. If, as the quarter draws to a close, one salesperson has a large lead, the other salespersons are likely to put off sales for the start of the next quarter. And, as they do this, the leader, seeing no one is catching up, does the same. On the other hand, if as the quarter draws to a close two or more salespersons are neck and neck . . . well . . . it will be Ford versus Honda for Sales Leader of the Year all over again. Of course, this might be a good thing, motivating the two leaders to ever greater efforts. But if they chase the prize by giving clients special deals, making promises on behalf of the organization that the organization might not want to keep, or cutting the price, it could be a very bad thing.

The way to avoid these problems is clear: The formula that transforms results into compensation should be "smooth"—avoid jumps—and should rise continuously—with no flat spots, please. Constant commission rates on sales are a good example. Or, in the context of Safelite, consider a scheme where the hourly wage is cut from $12 an hour to, say, $8 an hour, but in addition Safelite pays each technician $13 per windshield installed. A technician who works 40 hours in a week then starts with a base weekly "salary" of $320; 10 windshields done adds $130, for a total of $450. To get to the old level of $480 per week, the technician must install 13 windshields, which (we might hope) is within reach, and the technician maintains some incentive to push beyond that. You can adjust the $8 per hour down and the $13 per windshield up or vice versa (as long as you don't run afoul of minimum-wage laws, of course)—this is just trading off "insurance" against "incentive"—but the point is that this scheme maintains some incentive to perform throughout the range of possible outcomes.

You might also seek to avoid these problems by shortening the review period. At Safelite, for instance, change from a weekly to a daily review period: the technician is paid on a daily basis the greater of $30 times the number of windshields installed that day, or $96 (as long as he is on the job for the full eight hours). This can be especially effective—in theory—when the review period is so short that the individual doesn't know near the end of the period how well he did early in the period. However (a) this typically adds "noise," insofar as performance in the short run is more subject to randomness than longer-run performance, where the law of averages can kick in, (b) it can induce other dynamic problems—imagine an employee who comes to work on Monday a bit hung over and who decides to take it easy that day, or imagine an employee who has been quite successful the first four days of the week and decides to coast on Friday—and (c) for psychological reasons, people (including employees) are averse to continual review of their performance. So, overall, this in-theory cure is often worse than the problem it seeks to address.

The Ratchet Effect

A fairly common pay-for-performance scheme involves benchmarking the performance of an employee or a group of employees against how well they did last year or month or against how well they did in the best previous year or month. In the money-management industry (e.g., in hedge funds), for instance, compensation typically takes the form of a percentage of the money under management, plus a performance fee based on how well the fund's portfolio has done over its previous high-water mark, with no performance bonus if the portfolio is underwater. A production manager (or the production team) can be rewarded on how much progress they have achieved in lowering unit production costs. The manager of a branch office of a bank can be rewarded on the improvement shown in the branch's bottom or top line.

There are certainly cases in which this form of incentive pay is appropriate. For instance, Toyota Motor Manufacturing (Toyota in the United States) expects its suppliers to show continual cost improvements. A hedge-fund manager is expected to enhance the market value of her portfolio regardless of how the market is doing. (In contrast, a money manager whose investment strategy is "to beat the market" is more appropriately rewarded based on her fund's abnormal performance relative to the market benchmark appropriate to her portfolio.)

But this sort of incentive scheme is too often applied to situations where it doesn't work well, because of the so-called *ratchet effect*. Imagine a salesperson whose bonus is based on how much more he sells this year than he sold last. Suppose this salesperson has a spectacular year. He may get a great bonus this year, but he knows that he has ratcheted up his performance target for next year. Perhaps this will motivate him to look for a new and fresh start with a different employer.

And these sorts of incentive schemes can interact with dynamic effects in adverse ways. The salesperson who is having a spectacular year and who, in consequence, is thinking about leaving, will at the end of the year have extra incentive to pad his final year's sales figure by whatever means are available. On the other hand, the manager of a portfolio at a hedge fund who is underwater late in the year and who suspects she is about to be let go has the incentive to take gambles in her investment choices: Since she is underwater, she faces no downside risk, while if her gambles pay off, she might get over her high-water mark and earn a bonus.

To reiterate, these sorts of incentive schemes can be effective in settings where the technology of work makes improvement in outcomes an appropriate (albeit noisy) measure of the employee's (or employees') efforts. Outside of such contexts, they should be used with care.

Multitasking

Safelite moved to PPP, the modified piece-rate pay system, because it wanted to motivate its technicians to work more quickly. The main effect here was to lower unit labor costs; there is (as earlier noted) also a consumer-satisfaction element in motivating speed, as this means getting the client's car back on the road more quickly.

But there are other dimensions of "performance" in the job of a technician. Safelite wants its technicians to be courteous to clients. Safelite wants the technician to do a thorough job of vacuuming up any broken glass. It wants technicians going to and from a job to drive in a safe manner. A technician who does not take sufficient care in installing a windshield may cause the windshield to crack upon installation. For a subset of technicians—the lead technicians at each facility—it wants them to take time to train new technicians.

Insofar as Safelite is motivating speed, measured by the number of jobs completed each week, it is *de*-motivating each of these other desirable dimensions of performance. So, as part of an effective incentive regime, Safelite found that it had to move things around, to remotivate these other dimensions. For instance, they motivated better customer service by a different scheme of incentive pay, based on customer-satisfaction surveys. To motivate safe driving, they may have followed a common industry practice and put "How is my driving—Report dangerous driving to [phone number]" stickers on the back of its trucks, with the clear threat that a technician who generates irate calls about his driving will shortly be an ex-technician. As for glass that breaks upon installation, technicians did not get credit for the job; they could have strengthened this incentive even further if technicians also had to pay for the broken glass out of their compensation. (Although, if Safelite does this, it must be extra careful that the glass it hands out is not defective.)

The issue here is *multitasking*. Jobs typically involve a variety of tasks, and the performance of each task can be measured along a variety of dimensions. The employee must choose how to divide his time and effort among the different tasks, and he must decide how much time and attention to give to the different dimensions of a given task. Incentive schemes in most cases do a poor job at balancing the incentives they give to employees in making these choices. They tend to focus on a subset of the tasks and, for each task, on a subset of the dimensions of quality. And by employing a particular incentive scheme, the employer is sending the unmistakable signal that "since this is what I reward, this is what I want."

Two stories illustrate how difficult it can be to get it right when you try to motivate a multitasking employee with a pay-for-performance formula. The first involves incentives provided to analysts in a boutique hedge fund.[4] The founder and manager of the fund, Teena Lerner, had four analysts, each of whom covered a different segment of the health-care industry. She wished to provide them with incentives to provide her with the best possible advice, but she also wanted to motivate them to share information with one another. So she devised a formula for their year-end bonus payments that tied their bonus to how well their portfolios did and to how well the fund as a whole did; the latter to give them incentive to cooperate with one another. It was not a particularly complex formula but, because it tried to motivate two different things at the same time, it provided the analysts with some particularly perverse incentives. For instance, an analyst could find himself in a position where adding to his portfolio a position that had a negative expected return (and no correlation with other parts of anyone's portfolio) would increase his expected bonus. Without going into the details, the point is: Formula-driven reward schemes, even relatively simple ones, that try to do two or more things at once don't always work as the boss would want;

the interactions buried inside the formula can lead to unintended and undesirable consequences.

So, it would seem, the answer is to keep bonus formulas simple. But that raises a different sort of difficulty. The founder-CEOs of a chain of healthy-diet lunch shops once tried to motivate the managers of their different locations with a simple formula: Managers would get a percentage of the net profits earned by their location.[5] They tested this compensation/bonus scheme on two locations and discovered that the two managers involved went in entirely different directions: One manager decided to try to raise her profits by increasing her top line of sales revenue, building her business in a fashion that the CEOs heartily endorsed. But the other felt that, given his particular background and skills, his best course of action to raise store profit (and increase his compensation) was to concentrate on cutting costs, including cutting costs in ways that would probably negatively affect the chain's overall brand image, such as firing one of the kitchen staff, leading to longer wait times for meals. Simple formulas, based on summary measures of how well overall the employee has done, give employees discretion in what to do, discretion that (of course) they will exercise in ways that leverage what they personally are best able to do. This may be fine when all that matters about how the job is done is the summary measure. But in cases in which how the job is done generates spillovers for the reputation of the whole organization, the outcome of this sort of incentive scheme may be very far from "fine."

Multitasking difficulties can be particularly vicious when a job combines tasks that are easy to measure with tasks that are hard and noisy to measure. Think, for instance, of the job of the teacher of a fourth-grade class in a public school. The teacher has many tasks to which to attend, but limit your attention to the following two: bringing students in the class up to "grade-level" in reading and arithmetic skills; and inspiring students to love learning for its own sake. The first of these is relatively easy and noiseless to measure; students take a test at the end of the school year to see where they are. And, because teachers can't control the level at which their students begin the year, perhaps a test is given at the start of the school year, and the teacher is evaluated on the progress the students make. The second objective is, equally obviously, virtually impossible to measure in the near term. So, to motivate teachers to perform, they could be (and, to some extent, are) rewarded based on test performance. This has obvious consequences: Teachers who are evaluated and rewarded in this fashion, "teach to the test," ignoring or at least downplaying the inspirational aspects of their job.

If, in such cases, you don't want to dull incentives to do those tasks that are hard to measure, you can't strongly motivate tasks that are easy to measure, even though the tools to motivate those tasks are available. Hence, in jobs that by design mix hard- and easy-to-measure tasks, where you want the employee to spend time and effort on both types, pay for performance has limited value. As you engage in job design, you should keep this in mind, avoiding (whenever possible) roles that mix tasks that differ in this respect.

Subjective Evaluation Ex Post

The problems raised by multitasking usually become stronger the more complex the job, the more creativity and outside-the-box thinking desired, and the more ambiguous *ex ante* the tasks that need to be done. Our focus on Type-K jobs runs us directly up against these problems; all the features that make a job Type-K are features that, due to multitasking, make pay for performance particularly difficult, at least where the incentive pay is formulaically determined based on "objective" measures of performance.

Often, the fix for all these difficulties is to resort to *ex post* subjective reviews of performance: Rather than measure concrete outcomes and give a bonus that is determined by some formula, the boss—or some committee of bosses—looks subjectively at how each employee did *ex post* and decides what bonus the employee is given. In complex job situations, formulas rarely work and often are dysfunctional, so subjective *ex post* evaluation is about the only viable alternative for administering pay for performance. But such schemes give rise to obvious problems:

1. They motivate employees to spend a lot of time and effort getting on the good side of the folks who will review their performance, rather than performing.

2. Employees are put in the position of trying to "guess" what the bonus committee is going to look at when making their subjective determination. A savings and loan institution in Arizona illustrates the point.[6] Branch managers negotiated with headquarters a long list of

annual personal goals, being told that, when it came time to determine their bonus, the bonus committee would look at how well the manager did relative to the goals set at the start of the year. The list of goals was long, and achieving good results on one might require actions that directly compromised another. So managers had to figure out what "really" would matter. Not that they were left entirely in the dark: Headquarters was quite vocal about one category of goals for the first half of the year, and then shifted its emphasis midway through the year to a second category. You can guess the outcome: Branch managers seemed to ignore, or at least pay little attention to, activities not on the "front burner," with some particularly unhappy results in terms of the bank's financial performance.

3. And such schemes can and often do lead to disgruntled employees, who suspect that the bonus committee is either playing favorites or failing to recognize properly the distinctive contributions of the individual.

The bottom line is that the more complex the job in terms of the number of tasks and the number of dimensions of quality for those tasks, the less effective economic incentives can become, because the harder it is to balance incentives for the different tasks and their dimensions.

Screening Effects

A benefit to Safelite of its incentive scheme was that it not only motivated individual technicians to work faster, but also differentially motivated different types of employee and prospective employee, thereby improving the average quality of the population of technicians employed by Safelite. As noted before, careful measurement of the impact of the incentive scheme led to the conclusion that it caused unit labor costs to fall by around 30%, and fully *half* of that improvement was due to an improvement in the quality of technicians employed.

The point is obvious but important: The way you compensate your employees triggers different reactions in different types of employee, and so it changes the characteristics of those who choose to work for you and who stay on the job. Economists call this a *screening* effect.

Screening effects can be so strong that they can become the basis for a firm's business strategy. A great example of this is RE/MAX, the large American real-estate brokerage firm. Traditionally, realtors working for a large agency receive a base wage and a fraction of the commissions they generate from purchase and sale of properties, in return for which the agency provides offices, clerical assistance, and so forth. RE/MAX turned this on its head: Agents at RE/MAX can keep 100% of any commissions they generate, and they pay RE/MAX for the office space, clerical support, and so forth that they receive.* And, in fact, they pay

---

* RE/MAX offers prospective agents options on this basic scheme, options that offer a measure of insurance and that, therefore, probably dull the screening effect to some extent. See https://sites.google.com/site/joinrhe/compensation-plans.

RE/MAX more for these things than they would have to pay if they bought equivalent services on their own; RE/MAX profits from the difference in what its agents pay for these services and what it costs to provide the services.

Why are RE/MAX agents willing to pay this extra? Because, by doing so, they are labeled as RE/MAX agents, which is a valuable label. Within the population of all real estate agents, RE/MAX agents are known for having one or both of two characteristics: they are (a) more talented in their abilities to make deals, or (b) willing to work harder to make more deals. If you, as a buyer or seller of a house, want a realtor who is more likely to have qualities a and b, and you don't know of a particular agent with these characteristics, RE/MAX is the place to find one.

The reason the RE/MAX label persists as a strong signal for qualities a and b is due to the screening effects of the RE/MAX compensation scheme. This scheme is attractive to agents who know that they have characteristics a or b or both. It is unattractive to agents who aren't willing or able to work as hard or as well. Of course, agents who don't have characteristics a or b would still like the label RE/MAX agent, and the signal it provides, but the price they have to pay—taking the RE/MAX compensation scheme—is too high a price for them. In other words, the RE/MAX compensation scheme, through the screening effects it naturally triggers, is the foundation of RE/MAX's business strategy.

Recall the conversation about the basic trade-off in incentive theory: incentive versus risk shielding. RE/MAX goes to the extreme of no risk shielding at all for its agents. Therefore, besides

---

Recap: The Economic Theory of Incentives

Basic Idea: Pay more for better performance

Problem in Implementation: Measurable outcomes are usually a noisy indication of effort, leading to

The Fundamental Trade-Off: Incentives versus Insurance

Complications and Elaborations:
- Motivating malfeasance
- Eliminating extraneous risk
- Improving "insurance"
- Benchmarking and tournaments
- Interdependence and team-based incentives
- Dynamics
- The ratchet effect
- Multitasking
- Subjective evaluation *ex post*
- Screening effects

---

characteristics a and b, RE/MAX agents as a group tend to be less risk averse, whether because they have fewer financial obligations to meet (such as a family to feed) or they have more financial resources to call upon during a dry spell or simply because they are less bothered by risks. Having an agent who is more willing to gamble for the big payoff is not necessarily desirable for the client. So this is a less desirable aspect of being labeled a RE/MAX agent. But, on balance, a and b are desirable enough characteristics to be perceived as having, to overcome this.

Of course, a *personal* reputation for characteristics a and b, if widely known, is just as good as and perhaps even better than the label *RE/MAX agent*, and it doesn't involve overpaying for office space and clerical support. So, one expects, successful RE/MAX agents, as they gain a personal reputation with a clientele, are more likely to go off on their own and establish their own agencies. And, in fact, the data support this hypothesis.

The economic theory of incentives covers a lot of ground; see the recap on the previous page.

Stock Options: Incentive Theory or Something Different?

Stock options have been a very popular form of compensation in Silicon Valley (and elsewhere) in the relatively recent past, rationalized (in part) as a tool to motivate employee performance. Now that we've discussed incentive theory, it is useful to ask, *Does incentive theory explain the prevalence of options as compensation, or do options represent something different in the toolkit of motivational devices?*

Typically, stock options work as follows: Employees are periodically granted a number of stock options. These represent the right to buy shares of the company's common stock (equity) at a fixed price, called the strike price, which most often is the price of equity on the day the rights were granted. That is, for some period of time after the rights are granted, the employee can exercise his rights: He pays the company this fixed price (per right that he is exercising) and gets in return shares of stock in the company. If he was granted 100 rights, he can exercise however many—say 50—of them, paying fifty times the strike price set when the rights were granted him for fifty shares of the stock, worth (of course) whatever they are worth in the market today.

Typically, there are limitations to these rights: There can be a "vesting period," or a period that must pass before the right to buy shares can be exercised. If the employee leaves the company, any unexercised rights must be exercised over some short time frame or are lost. And, even if the employee remains at the company, there may be some date after which the rights, if not yet exercised, expire.

These are called "options" because the employee has the option whether and when to exercise his rights.* Consider options granted to an individual employee on September 1, 2010, with a strike price of $15, which was the market price of the firm's equity that day. Suppose that these options have a vesting period of five years—they cannot be exercised before September 1, 2015—but must be exercised by some stipulated date, say, no later than August 31, 2025. Within that window, the employee must decide whether and when to exercise his options. He will never (rationally) exercise them when the price of a share of the company's stock is below the strike price of $15; he must write a check for $15 to get a share of stock, and if the price of the stock

---

* The use of the term "option" is a bit imprecise. While it is true that the employee can choose within some limits when and whether to exercise his rights to buy shares, in financial markets, the term "option" is generally used to describe a security in zero net supply. When and if the employee exercises one of these options-cum-compensation, the company creates new shares of common stock, diluting the value of existing shares. The proper financial term for this sort of financial instrument is *warrants*.

is $13, he can go to the market, buy a share for $13, and retain his options.* But if, say, on October 18, 2020, the price of the stock is $35, he must decide whether to exercise: If he does, he can turn around and make a net profit of $20 per right he exercises—he has paid $15 for a share of stock worth $35, which means he can sell his share for that price—or he can exercise some or all of his options and hold the stock, if he thinks that the price of the stock will go even higher. Of course, if he thinks the price is on the rise, he could just as easily buy some shares and retain his options: The current stock price of $35 presumably reflects at least some chance that the price of the stock will go below $15, and no one can force him to exercise his options in such circumstances. So maybe it is better to wait to exercise. There are complications arising from taxes and dividends the company may pay, and we must take into account the possibility that he might offset his position in options by buying a put option on the open market; you must consult a book on trading in options to get the full picture of what he might do with his options. But the point is, they are something valuable, whose value is tied to the price of the firm's common stock.

Besides the restrictions—the vesting period, the length of time the options can be exercised, what happens if the employee leaves the firm—mentioned above, there are tax considerations to take into account: Options are part of the employee's compensation, so the tax code determines when and how much income or

---

* This argument assumes the individual can freely purchase shares in the market. If he has inside information that the company is worth more than its current market price, he might be barred from purchasing shares by insider-trading rules but allowed to exercise options he holds. In which case, he might exercise options even when the market price is below the strike price.

capital gains tax he must pay and when. And there are rules concerning how the granting of options affects the company's income statement, both for reporting and for tax purposes. All of which is made more complex by the fact that, under law, there are two types of options—incentive stock options and nonqualified stock options—that are treated differently.

I will not go into any of these details but instead pose the question, *Why would a company and employee ever agree to such a forbiddingly complex form of compensation? Why not just pay cash?* If you made a list of reasons why stock options were popular, say, around the year 2000, the list would have featured:

1. For a start-up that is cash constrained, this is a form of compensation that doesn't consume cash.

2. In 2000, firms did not have to recognize the option grant to an employee as an expense on its income statement, making it look healthier. In some cases, this could allow the firm to finance continued operations on better terms.

3. Especially in the very active job market of Silicon Valley, but also in general, firms looked for schemes that would fix employees (reduce voluntary turnover), and features of options such as the loss of as-yet unvested options and the six-months-to-exercise-if-you-leave features increased the cost to an employee of departing.

Explanations 1 and 3 continue to hold; Explanation 2 no longer holds because rules for financial accounting (as promulgated by the Federal Accounting Standards Board [FASB] in the United States, and by similar bodies outside the United States) now mandates that option grants be valued and reported as a current expense.* But, then, and still today, the story most often told involves day-to-day motivation of the employee:

4. Options align the interests of the employee with those of the organization. The employee, owning an option to buy for a set price shares in the firm, would be motivated to take steps to increase the value of the firm's equity.

This sounds at first like an application of the economic theory of incentives but, from the perspective of the theory, this story doesn't make a huge amount of sense. Think it through for two categories of employee:

A. For most employees, their individual efforts in support of the company and its strategy have little impact on the price of equity of the company. From their perspective, compensation based on the price of the company's common stock is very risky in a manner over which they have very little control. Worse still, to the extent that the returns on their human capital—the salaries or wages they will earn in the future—are tied up in

---

* Explanation 2 can still hold, albeit with reduced force, if FASB's rule for how stock options must be expensed combined with the value the employee puts on the options relative to cash makes the granting of options a cheaper alternative to paying cash.

the fortunes of the company for which they work, the risks of compensation that track the price of equity in the firm are compounded. As an incentive device, then, grants of stock options would seem to have gotten the risk versus incentive trade-off completely wrong: lots of risk, for extremely little direct incentive.

B. Top managers of the firm, on the other hand, may through their efforts on the job have considerable influence on the price of equity of the firm. For such managers, the risk-incentive trade-off makes some sense. But (at least) two second-order considerations arise for these folks.

   Suppose the company in the example given a few paragraphs prior is struggling, with a price of equity around $10. Suppose the CEO holds a lot of options with a strike price of $15. At an equity price of $10, these options aren't worthless: If she (the CEO) could sell them, she might get something for them, since it is always possible that the company will recover and its common stock price will get above $15. But they probably aren't worth much. And the act of selling out-of-the-money options is probably outside the rules (the rules often forbid selling options at all; either exercise them and sell the shares, or hold them). Even if permitted, the optics of a CEO selling off the options she holds in the company she runs are . . . not good. So, with all that non-wealth tied up in options, what are her incentives? They are, at least in part, to do what she can to get the price of the stock up above $15. From her perspective vis-à-vis these options, it doesn't matter to her if the price of the company's shares is $10 or $5 or $2. Her options are worth nothing in all three cases. So the options incline her to take gambles that *might* pay off and get the price of equity up to, say, $20, even if those gambles probably mean a price of equity down in the $2 range. This is just the *flat-spots* problem already discussed.

On the other hand, suppose top managers of the firm have a lot of their personal wealth tied to the fortunes of the firm. If they are personally risk averse, they may forgo taking risky investments that would be in the interests of their more diversified shareholders. Options allow them to benefit more from the upside than they lose on the downside, which might motivate them to take such risky investments.

And, to complicate matters still further, top management has many other incentive concerns weighing on them. To assert that options align their interests with those of the shareholders in the firm, at least in this sort of situation, is a good deal less than completely obvious.

So does the economic theory of incentives explain the prevalence of stock options as compensation? I don't believe so. Yet, despite this, and despite the disappearance of Reason 2 given above, options remain a fairly popular form of compensation for small firms. This could be a combination of Reasons 1 and 3 but, in fact, proponents of options—including options for employees well below the CEO suite in the organizational hierarchy—continue to assert that options are a tool for motivating employees. Something is going on here that is not explained by the economic theory of incentives.

3

Is Pay for Performance Always "The Answer?"

Pay for performance, in the form of piece-rate pay or year-end bonuses or, more generally, any rewards for performance, can be a powerful motivational tool. That is clearly shown in the case of Safelite. But, as the other anecdotes from the last chapter make clear, for jobs more complex than that of Safelite technician, pay for performance can be difficult to get right; and it may even be dysfunctional.

You, presumably, are interested in answers to the following questions:

1. Is pay for performance the answer in your particular situation?

2. If not, why not?

3. If not, what are the alternatives?

Matching the characteristics of last chapter's anecdotes to your particular situation may give you a hint concerning the answer to Question 1, but it would be nice to have systematically collected evidence. Ideally, one would want to conduct controlled experiments: In a variety of contexts, compare pay for performance with alternatives (that is, once we have some idea what are the alternatives), and see which is more effective where.

I can't provide you with such ideal evidence, because it is hard to get organizations to permit experiments on how they motivate their employees. We could try to find a sample of firms that vary on how they motivate their employees and, after controlling for observable differences, see how they perform, relative to one another. But research of this sort is rarely conclusive or trustworthy.*

What I can do is to tell you what a variety of senior executives think about motivation in their organizations. As part of my duties at Stanford GSB, I have taught in a six-week, open-enrollment, general-management program called the Stanford Executive Program (SEP). The participants come from around the globe, they are fairly senior in their organizations, and they come from a variety of industries and functions. Over the past few years, I've surveyed them about motivation. Response rates have been around 60%; demographics of the 207 respondents from the summers or 2014 and 2015 are given in Table 1.

---

* One thing that makes research of this sort difficult to trust has the technical name of *endogeneity*. Firms presumably choose their motivation schemes based on their specific context (strategy) and environment. Researchers can say that they are "controlling for observable differences" among firms in their sample, but the adjective "observable" in that phrase is there for a reason.

Table 1. Demographics of the SEP Survey Respondents

Domicile		Sex	
US/Canada	30.0%	Male	86.0%
Latin America	4.8%	Female	14.0%
Europe	28.0%	**Functional specialty**	
East/South Asia	22.2%	General management	45.4%
Middle East/Africa	2.9%	Finance	9.2%
Australia/NZ/Pacific Islands	12.1%	Accounting	0.5%
Age		Marketing	7.2%
Less than 40 years old	16.4%	Ops./prod./mfg.	6.3%
40 to 44 years old	33.3%	Information technology	8.2%
45 to 49 years old	30.9%	Human resource mgmt.	1.9%
50 to 54 years old	14.5%	Strategic planning	5.8%
55 years old or older	4.8%	Other	15.5%
Organizational rank		**Industry**	
Chair/CEO/managing partner/president	21.3%	Financial services/investments	17.9%
		Information technology	23.2%
COO	4.3%	Manufacturing/construction	14.5%
Head of staff function: CFO/CPO/CIO/etc.	19.3%	Health care/pharma/biotech	7.7%
		Marketing/retail	6.3%
Senior VP/senior partner	11.1%	Public sector	5.8%
VP/partner	19.3%	Consulting/advisory/education	5.3%
General manager	24.6%	Other	19.3%

The survey asks a variety of questions—it is described in detail in the appendix—but for these purposes, the money questions are

Consider the following five motivational channels:

- Personal and tangible rewards linked to the achievement of good outcomes, such as bonuses or promotion.

- Personal intangible rewards, such as praise or enhanced status/respect among co-workers, linked to the achievement of good outcomes.

- The opportunity to do work that is interesting and/or exciting to the employee.

- A clear connection between the achievement of good individual outcomes and success of the organization or workgroup.

- The opportunity to do work that is socially important.

Which of these five channels is MOST descriptive of what motivates your own best work? Which is MOST descriptive of what motivates the best work of your direct reports?

When it comes to motivating their own best work, 27.5% of the respondents said contributing to success of the organization and 25.6% said interesting and exciting work is most descriptive, while only 15.4% said tangible personal rewards. For their direct reports, 26.6% said exciting and interesting work, 23.6% said contributing to organizational success, and only 17.4% said tangible personal rewards.

Forcing the survey respondents to pick one *most* descriptive motivational channel doesn't necessarily give a full picture of their opinions about the effectiveness of each. So I also asked them to rate each of the five motivational channels on a six-point scale: not at all effective; of limited effectiveness; effective but not very effective; very effective; extremely effective; and only this channel is effective. The full results are shown in Table 2, where I also compute average or mean scores (where not at all effective = 1, etc.), and the standard deviations of the scores. The full results show that, although tangible personal rewards—the stuff of pay for performance—are not ineffective, they lag significantly compared to interesting and exciting work, contributing to organizational success, and even intangible personal rewards.

The participants in SEP average 47 years old, and the median

Table 2. Responses from SEP Participants on the Five Motivational Channels

(a) Which channel is most descriptive

	Tangible rewards; e.g., pay	Intangible personal rewards; e.g., praise	Interesting & exciting work	Contributes to organizational success	Contributes to greater social purpose
For self	15.5%	11.1%	25.6%	27.5%	20.3%
For direct reports	17.4%	20.2%	26.6%	23.7%	12.1%

(b) Self scores

	Tangible rewards; e.g., pay	Intangible personal rewards; e.g., praise	Interesting & exciting work	Contributes to organizational success	Contributes to greater social purpose
Not at all effective	0.5%	0.0%	0.0%	0.0%	1.0%
Limited effectiveness	6.3%	3.9%	0.5%	1.0%	10.6%
Effective, but not very	30.9%	17.9%	5.3%	6.8%	29.0%
Very effective	33.8%	41.5%	29.0%	32.4%	31.4%
Extremely effective	27.5%	32.4%	58.0%	52.7%	24.6%
Only this is effective	1.0%	4.3%	7.2%	7.2%	3.4%
Mean	3.85	4.15	4.66	4.58	3.78
Standard deviation	0.95	0.71	0.76	1.07	0.90

(c) Scores for direct reports

	Tangible rewards; e.g., pay	Intangible personal rewards; e.g., praise	Interesting & exciting work	Contributes to organizational success	Contributes to greater social purpose
Not at all effective	0.0%	0.0%	0.0%	0.0%	0.5%
Limited effectiveness	8.7%	1.0%	1.9%	2.9%	20.3%
Effective, but not very	29.0%	21.3%	4.8%	20.8%	40.1%
Very effective	40.1%	49.3%	37.7%	44.0%	25.6%
Extremely effective	21.3%	27.5%	51.2%	30.9%	13.0%
Only this is effective	1.0%	1.0%	4.3%	1.4%	0.5%
Mean	3.77	4.06	4.51	4.07	3.32
Standard deviation	0.91	0.75	0.74	0.83	0.97

participant in terms of rank is a senior VP/partner. Would we get similar results by surveying younger and less senior managers? I've conducted a very similar survey with students in the Stanford GSB's MBA program; the differences were that the MBA students were asked to discuss motivation on their last job before enrolling, and instead of their direct reports they were asked to discuss their peers at their last job. My survey was spread across two years of students who were enrolled in a course on HRM that I taught in the spring quarters of 2014 and 2015. I received 240 responses, representing an 80% response rate, so this is fairly representative of the MBA population (or, at least, that segment that chose to take a course in HRM). The demographics for the respondents are in Table 3, and their responses to the five-channel questions are in Table 4.

Perhaps the most noticeable difference in the responses of these two groups is the extent to which contributing to success of the organization matters. For the SEP participants, it is virtually the leader for themselves and a strong second-place for their direct reports; for the MBA students, it is arguably tied for last place. And, at least as regards their own motivation, the median MBA student identifies intangible personal rewards such as praise as being extremely effective.*

The differences in responses in these two samples tell us that age and organizational rank "matter" in what motivates the individual and the people close to him or her in the organization. One can ask whether other demographic characteristics matter: Do, for instance, tangible personal rewards score more highly for people in

---

* The appendix will supply measures of statistical significance of these differences.

Table 3. Demographics of the MBA-Student Respondents

Domicile	
US/Canada	70.8%
Latin America	7.5%
Europe	8.3%
East/South Asia	7.1%
Middle East/Africa	5.0%
Australia/NZ/Pacific Islands	1.3%
Age	
25 years & younger	13.3%
26 to 30 years old	80.0%
31 years & older	6.7%
Sex	
Male	56.7%
Female	43.3%
College major	
Economics	20.8%
Business	16.7%
Other social science	14.2%
Engineering	21.3%
Biological sciences	7.1%
Physical sciences & math	5.8%
Humanities	14.2%

Functional specialty	
General management	25.4%
Finance	23.8%
Accounting	0.4%
Marketing	8.3%
Ops./prod./mfg.	5.4%
Information technology	1.3%
Human resource mgmt.	2.1%
Strategic planning	19.6%
Other	13.8%
Industry	
Financial services/investments	24.2%
Information technology	10.4%
Manufacturing/construction	4.2%
Health care/pharma/biotech	7.9%
Marketing/retail	5.0%
Public sector	6.7%
Consulting	20.4%
Education	4.2%
Not-for-profit/social enterprise	4.2%
Social media	0.4%
Entertainment	3.8%
Student just prior to GSB	0.4%
Other	8.3%

Table 4. MBA-Student Responses to the Five-Motivational-Channel Questions

(a) Which channel is most descriptive

	Tangible rewards; e.g., pay	Intangible personal rewards; e.g., praise	Interesting & exciting work	Contributes to organizational success	Contributes to greater social purpose
For self	14.6%	28.8%	37.9%	7.9%	10.8%
For peers	28.8%	22.1%	34.2%	4.6%	10.4%

(b) Self scores

	Tangible rewards; e.g., pay	Intangible personal rewards; e.g., praise	Interesting & exciting work	Contributes to organizational success	Contributes to greater social purpose
Not at all effective	0.4%	0.0%	0.4%	2.1%	5.0%
Limited effectiveness	7.5%	2.9%	0.8%	15.4%	13.8%
Effective, but not very	25.0%	9.6%	6.3%	25.4%	26.7%
Very effective	39.6%	32.1%	18.3%	35.0%	28.3%
Extremely effective	26.3%	52.5%	65.8%	20.8%	22.9%
Only this is effective	1.3%	2.9%	8.3%	1.3%	3.3%
Mean	3.88	4.43	4.73	3.61	3.60
Standard deviation	0.94	0.81	0.76	1.08	1.21

(c) Scores for peers

	Tangible rewards; e.g., pay	Intangible personal rewards; e.g., praise	Interesting & exciting work	Contributes to organizational success	Contributes to greater social purpose
Not at all effective	0.4%	0.0%	0.0%	2.5%	5.0%
Limited effectiveness	4.6%	1.7%	1.3%	19.6%	26.3%
Effective, but not very	20.8%	12.5%	9.6%	36.3%	30.0%
Extremely effective	33.8%	40.4%	49.2%	14.6%	10.4%
Only this is effective	1.7%	0.4%	4.2%	0.0%	0.4%
Mean	4.06	4.25	4.45	3.32	3.14
Standard deviation	0.95	0.74	0.83	1.02	1.10

the financial sector? How about men versus women? Or executives based in Europe versus those based in the United States or Canada?

The appendix provides detailed information about such demographic impacts; for current purposes, it is enough to say that these things do matter, at least to some extent: In terms of motivating one's own best work, tangible personal rewards are most descriptive for 14.6% of the respondents who are not in the financial sector versus 20% for those who are in the financial sector. And for direct reports, the percentages are 16.7% for those not in the financial sector versus 25% for those who are. A second and notable comparison involves individuals whose organizational rank puts them in the chair/CEO/president bucket: 33% of the respondents in that bucket say that contributing to organizational success is most descriptive of what motivates their best work; for those of lesser rank, the percentage is only 25.9%.

What can we conclude from these survey results? If we trust that the respondents are giving honest and accurate answers—and please do not prejudge that assumption; it's a topic to which we'll return in Chapter 6—then I think two obvious conclusions emerge:

1. There is no single answer to the question, *How does one motivate best effort?* If you examine Tables 2 and 4 closely, you might conclude that "interesting and exciting work" comes pretty close to a "one size fits all" motivator, but beyond that, there is a lot of variation in the answers given.

2. In particular, tangible personal rewards for performance is certainly not a "one size fits all" answer.

Given the back half of the previous chapter, the second conclusion shouldn't come as much of a surprise, given all the complications and limiting factors of pay for performance. But how do
we understand what does work? And, insofar as there is no single
answer—insofar as effective motivation must be tailored to the
specific work context—how can we think in systematic fashion
about the connection from context to effective motivation?

To answer this last question, and in particular to understand
what might be effective in the context of your organization, you
first must understand the employment relationship both as an
economic and as a social relationship.

If you've studied economics, the picture you are likely to have
in your mind of "economic relationships" is the hoary economic
model of supply equals demand. The economic theory that under-
pins pay for performance, in essence, is based on supply equals
demand. It conceives of employment as a discrete and one-time
transaction between employer and employee. The employer tells
the employee, "This is how your compensation will be determined." And the employee then chooses whether to take the job
at all and, if so, how hard to work and on what tasks.

In some contexts, that model of employment works well. But
in cases where employment is not a one-time transaction but an
enduring relationship between employer and employee, we must
rethink the nature of the "transaction," both in terms of the economic and the social exchange. So, fasten your seatbelts: For
the next two chapters, we explore employment, and specifically
employment relationships, in both economic and social terms.

4

The Economics of Employment Relationships

L et's begin our exploration of employment relationships with a concrete, though concocted, example of employee Bob working for employer Zephyr Corporation.

Bob and Zephyr

Imagine someone—call him Bob—who last year took a job with an organization I'll call Zephyr Corporation. Bob was a civil-engineering major in college, and his job with Zephyr, a global infrastructure-construction firm, is his first postcollege job. Bob is an ambitious sort—he anticipates at some point going back to school, perhaps to get an MBA—so, when he interviewed for jobs as he was finishing college, he didn't know how long he would work for his first employer. But he felt that a few years of practical experience would stand him in good stead in the long run, help build a résumé that would be attractive to business school admissions officers, *and* give him the opportunity to have some fun and make a bit of money.

At the outset, Bob knew *basically* what the job at Zephyr would entail, at least for a while. The recruiter from Zephyr sketched the first few months and even years, as follows. Bob would begin with a four-week uptake program, in which he would learn about administrative and work processes at Zephyr. He would next be assigned to an overseas-project team at which he would take day-to-day direction from his team leader concerning specific tasks to be done. He would live on-site at the project, and he could expect this first assignment to last for a year to eighteen months. If he does well, he was told, he will probably next be assigned to a new team in a new location and, at some point, if he continues to do well, he will be promoted to the position of team leader. He was also told that Zephyr's general policy is to send employees out on overseas assignments for their first three years with the firm but, after that, they can opt for posting at a domestic project and even to be more-or-less permanently located at one of Zephyr's domestic offices. But, the recruiter told him, promotion prospects are greater for employees who are willing to continue to take overseas postings: "The route to real advancement at Zephyr," the recruiter said, "is to supervise larger and more significant projects, which tend to be in remote parts of the world." Bob asked whether recruits at Zephyr had the ability to take time off to continue their studies and whether Zephyr might support such study; the recruiter hemmed and hawed about this and ultimately gave the vague answer, "It depends. It happens, sometimes."

All this sounded agreeable to Bob in a general sort of way. Of course, a lot of details remained to be filled in, such as where his

first posting would be, who would be his boss, and what exactly
he would be working on. And there was Bob's hanging question
about further education. But Bob didn't really expect, and the
recruiter couldn't supply, those specifics. When Bob considered
this job offer, he had offers from several other firms, who made
similar but not identical pitches. He took Zephyr's offer because
Zephyr offered a good salary package with the promise of annual
year-end bonuses, and because the general idea of going overseas
had a lot of appeal to Bob. He checked with folks who know the
industry; they told him that Zephyr had a good reputation as an
employer. It sounded like a good (if somewhat vague) deal to him,
so he signed up and went out to celebrate.

Bob, Zephyr, and Economics

This story illustrates the following general characteristic of long-
term employment:

- Long-term employment constitutes an ongoing relationship between employer and employee, a relationship
  whose *exact* terms of trade—what the employee will be
  doing years and perhaps even months hence—are determined only as time passes. There may be some general
  principles and company policies about how the relationship will unfold, but few concrete and specific promises
  given, just somewhat vague verbal assurances that are
  not enforceable in court.

- In place of a detailed agreement about how the relationship will evolve, the job comes with a process by which its evolution—that is, the *What next?*—is determined: Bob understood that his assignments would be made by higher-ups at Zephyr, and his day-to-day duties would be determined by his project team leader(s). He knows that he can offer opinions about what he'd like, and he can hope that those opinions carry some weight with the decision maker(s). But, at least for some time, he will be *given* assignments; if he doesn't want to take what is given, his recourse is to quit Zephyr and look for a new job (or go back to school). As time passes, and if he is successful, he'll have more and more decision authority in determining what he does. But even if he someday becomes CEO, he will have a board of directors to which he must answer.

This "make it up as we go along" character isn't true of all employment relationships, and it varies in degree among those for which it is true. There is very little truth to this as a description of the job of a day laborer hired to perform some specific manual labor. A limited-term contract employee is nearly the same as the day laborer. Someone going to work as an analyst for, say, a consulting firm will have a reasonably predictable work life, at least for a while. But the more the word "relationship" applies in a particular employment relationship, the more we have a situation like Bob and Zephyr, in which *What next?* is not fixed from the outset but only resolved as events unfold.

How did things work out for Bob? His first posting was to a project in southern India, near Chennai, and his team leader was Alice. Eleven months in, Bob was increasingly convinced that he didn't get along with Alice and that he didn't like the climate of Chennai. He was, therefore, hoping to be reassigned to another team in another, more temperate part of the world. But notwithstanding his personal problems with Alice, he did good work for her, and she put in a strong request that Bob continue to work on her team for at least six more months. In the end, Bob was told that, notwithstanding his request to be moved to another project, he would spend at least the next six months in Chennai, working for Alice. But, he was told, if he continued his strong performance, his request for a different posting would be given all due consideration after the six months were up.

Bob was not happy about this, but he was told this decision was final. Of course, he had the option of quitting Zephyr. So he considered the costs and benefits of doing so. The costs included: He would be without work, at least for a while, searching for a new job. Whatever jobs he applied for (or, if he decided to apply for graduate study) would presumably want letters of reference from Alice. He suspected that she knew he wasn't a big fan, and he was worried what she might write. He had made some good friends in the company, and he continued to believe that, in the longer run, working for Zephyr would be good for him and his résumé. And he had invested time and effort in acquiring both knowledge about and a good track record at Zephyr; quitting after a year would throw much of that investment away. If he were aggrieved enough about being stuck in Chennai with Alice, he might have been willing to pay these costs. But since it was only (probably) six months more, he decided to stick it out and hope for better at the next iteration.

Bob's situation illustrates a third important characteristic of long-term employment relationships:

- Once the relationship has begun, and usually increasingly as time passes, the employee has assets at risk. If the employee is dissatisfied with the job, he can quit. But doing so forfeits, at least for a while and perhaps permanently, items that are valuable to the employee: a steady paycheck; perhaps a good recommendation for the next job; good friends that have been acquired. For employees with families, seeking a new job may mean relocating, disrupting the employment of a significant other or the schooling of children.

Because Bob has these assets at risk—because it will be costly for him to walk away from his job—he is the victim of a *holdup* (which, believe it or not, is the technical term used by economists to describe this situation). Management at Zephyr knew that Bob, like other employees, faced these costs of quitting—the technical term is *transaction costs*—and they knew that they could, in consequence, take advantage of him to some extent, keeping him at a posting where he was valuable to the company, even if it was not the posting he wanted.

But understand that while Bob has assets at risk, so does Zephyr. Bob has gained experience at Zephyr and, even more significantly, he has become knowledgeable about the project on which he is working. Therefore, Zephyr's next best alternative to dealing with Bob is not as good as keeping Bob on the job. If the gap in values to Zephyr between keeping Bob in Chennai and their next best alternative is wide enough, maybe Bob can turn things around and hold up Zephyr by telling them, "If I'm so valuable to you on this project, give me an immediate bonus. If you don't, I'll quit." If Zephyr believes Bob will quit without this bonus, and if the size of the bonus is less than the gap for Zephyr between having Bob and not, Zephyr might well decide that it is prudent to pay.*

This is why supply equals demand isn't the right economic model. What drives supply equals demand is that every market participant has a nearly-as-good alternative; namely, to transact with another buyer or seller at virtually the same price, for virtually the same good. In a market where this condition is met, neither buyer nor seller can hold up the other side. Neither side can say "For you, I'm the uniquely best trading partner you have— better by a nontrivial amount than your next best alternative—and I will use that fact to extract some extra value (money) from you."

Contrast Bob's situation with my relationship with my grocer: For many years, I bought most of my groceries at a local family owned and operated supermarket. The relationship that I had with the owners of this grocery was open-ended, just like Bob's relationship with Zephyr: I didn't know what I would buy six days, let alone six months, hence, and they gave me no guarantees what prices they would be charging in the future, or whether they would continue to carry the particular cuts of meat that I would

---

* If you are thinking that Zephyr won't give in to these demands, because they don't want to acquire a reputation for being a soft touch, you are already where we are headed. Read on.

want. And if they kept an inventory of those particular cuts of meat, they had no assurance that I'd show up to buy. But if, one day, I decided that the relationship was no longer working for me, the cost of transferring my business to the local Safeway would be trivial. And if I failed to show up, there would be plenty of other customers for them to serve, some of who would be happy to buy what I did not. Hence, supply equals demand, applied day by day, works as an economic model in this case.

And supply equals demand would be an adequate model if, from the outset, Bob and Zephyr could put in place contractual guarantees for *What next?* over the duration of his employment. At the moment he was comparing jobs, he didn't have assets at risk; if he knew (and could guarantee) exactly what would transpire for as long as he worked for Zephyr, he could (at least, according to economic theory) compare the Zephyr job offer with others and make a free choice. If Zephyr could lock in exactly what Bob would do, they could decide whether to make him an offer and on what terms.

It is the combination of the incomplete or open-ended nature of the relationship and the fact that, once the relationship is consummated, parties have assets at risk, that takes us away from supply equals demand.

If supply equals demand is not the right economic model, what is? For enduring employment relationships, economists have come to rely instead on a model based on three interrelated concepts: governance, credibility, and reputation.

Governance

Governance refers to the rules that govern how the relationship evolves; essentially, it comes down to which parties are allowed—either formally or informally—to make various decisions about, *What next?*

In some cases, called *hierarchical* governance, one of the parties involved in the transaction makes most of the *What-next?* decisions. For instance, and in a very different context, Toyota outsources to subcontractors the manufacture of many major subassemblies that go into its cars, on the basis of ongoing relationships with those subcontractors. The formal contract between Toyota and each subcontractor is very short and succinct; in particular, the contract specifies neither the quantities Toyota will buy nor the prices Toyota will pay past the first few months of the contract. Instead, Toyota, by convention that is completely understood by both parties to the relationship, makes these decisions on a take-it-or-leave-it basis. A subcontractor reserves the right to quit at any time. But, having invested in their relationship with Toyota, subcontractors rarely quit. This, of course, makes them very susceptible to a holdup. We'll explain what protects the subcontractors—and moreover gives them the motivation to invest in their relationship with Toyota—shortly.[1] Traditionally, employment relationships are similarly governed: The employer tells the employee what he will do on a day-to-day basis; the employee's options are to do what he is told or quit.

In other cases, decision-making authority is shared. Sometimes, the rule is that there is a status quo, and it takes consent by both parties to change the status quo. Or, if no agreement is reached, the relationship simply dissolves. In other cases, different parties have decision rights over different specific decisions; for instance, one party (the seller, say) decides on the price to be paid; the second party (the buyer) decides on how much to buy at that price. In the context of employment, this sort of *bilateral governance* is observed in particular when employees are represented by a union.

And in still other cases, decision-making authority is vested in some third and supposedly neutral party. An example is a labor agreement between a corporation and a labor union in which disputes are settled by binding arbitration by a panel of neutral labor experts. In some cases, the arbitrators are free to propose a compromise. In other cases, the rules of arbitration state that the two principal parties must state their alternative positions, and the arbitrators are constrained to pick one or the other of these. Governance in which a third and supposedly neutral party is part of the picture is called *trilateral*.

These three forms of governance are ideal or pure forms. In real-life examples, you nearly always have a mix. For instance, even in the most hierarchical employment situation, where the employer tells the employee what to do, the employee retains the right to quit.

How are these decision rights determined? In some cases, it is a matter of law. To give an obvious example: Laws against slavery and indenture provide all employees with the right to quit at will (although noncompete clauses in employment contracts sometimes limit what the employee can do after quitting). Contract law, and labor law in particular, provide further limitations on how decision rights are assigned; for instance, an employer cannot compel an employee to take illegal actions or fire an employee who refuses to do so.

In other cases, decision rights are assigned contractually, as in "take-or-pay" clauses between a vendor and its customers. In employment contexts, decision rights can be the subject of formal negotiation by the parties involved, especially when employees are organized into a union. (And, when unions are involved, there are legal restrictions on the agreements that labor and management can reach.)

But perhaps most often, decision rights are a matter of mutual understanding: Subcontractors to Toyota understand the way Toyota does business, namely Toyota calls nearly all the shots. This is never explicitly stated, and it certainly isn't part of the formal contract between Toyota and the subcontractor, which instead is an aspirational paean to cooperation, mutual agreement, and mutual benefit. But a company that wants to work with Toyota knows, if only through the grapevine, that it is Toyota's way or the highway. Or to return to Bob and Zephyr, Bob was told up front that he'd be given his first few assignments without discussion; when he accepted the job, he implicitly accepted that this was "how things are done at Zephyr."

Allocating Decision Rights Efficiently

A different but related question is, *Why are decision rights assigned as they are?* Why design a take-or-pay contract? Why does Toyota insist that it call the shots in its relationship with its subcontractors?

When it comes to legal restrictions on governance, we get a mix of "what lawmakers think is socially good" with interest-group politics. To give an example, Tesla, the automobile manufacturer, is legally barred from selling its cars in the state of Michigan. Instead, if it wants to sell cars in Michigan, it must set up an independent dealership network. The laws in this case were created long ago to protect the interests of independent dealers (and other franchise operations) from being held up by their upstream "partners"; today, the laws are maintained well beyond their original purpose by organized groups—in this case, dealership organizations in Michigan—because the laws benefit the group's members economically.

But beyond legal restrictions, governance is a matter of design and choice. In contracts, the parties negotiate over who decides what when it comes to *What next?*

In cases like Toyota or Zephyr, one party says, "This is what works for me, and if you want to deal with me, you should understand and agree." Of course, negotiating power and the desire to be in control play their parts here; Toyota gains from calling nearly all the shots, and prospective suppliers find it so desirable to form a relationship with Toyota that they agree to this arrangement. But, more than this, Toyota insists on this arrangement because it is *efficient*. Any assignment of decision rights has implications for how smoothly and well *What next?* will be determined and then implemented. Making good *What-next?* decisions and implementing them smoothly means a more valuable transaction overall, and more value means more for the parties to split between them. So, in particular, as you are thinking about what sort of governance provisions you want in your organization, you should be asking, What's the best, most efficient way to get to good decisions?

Start with *information and ability*: Which party is better able to formulate the "best" decision and which party has the best information pertinent to this decision? One reason for Toyota to call nearly all the shots is that Toyota is in the center of a large array of bilateral relationships, and it knows best about coordinating the activities of its many suppliers. Similarly, the classic model of employment—where the employer directs the activities of employees—is efficient because the employer specializes in understanding how to achieve coordination among her many employees.

Note, however, that when it comes to Type-K employees, the employer no longer knows what is best to do; it becomes efficient for the employee to choose what he does and how he does it. For instance, when I was associate dean of Stanford GSB, it made sense for me to tell faculty members which courses they would teach, in which quarters, on which days, and at which hours, because I had the job of coordinating the different course offerings available to students. (Of course, I asked faculty members for their preferences, which I tried to accommodate. But the final say belongs to the dean.) But it made no sense for me to tell my colleagues how to teach the courses to which they were assigned.

In many cases, neither party to a transaction has a monopoly on valuable information relevant to some particular decision. One party knows some things that are important; the second party knows other things, and the best decision emerges if they pool their information.

Toyota understands this and *still* it wants to call all the shots. So, in the day-to-day management of its relationships with its suppliers, Toyota spends a lot of time and money understanding in detail the inner workings of those suppliers. As dean, I always asked my faculty colleagues about their preferences and their constraints concerning what and when they would teach, and I tried, but only sometimes succeeded, in giving them what they requested. As employer, if there are decisions you want to be able to make concerning your employees' activities that are best made based on information that is naturally held by them, then it is your job—a crucial job—to spend time and effort learning enough of what they know, so you can make a good decision.

Credibility

If information and ability are crucial considerations when it comes to efficient governance, credibility is just as important. For an employment relationship to work well, decisions should be made by the party that can be trusted not to exploit their decision rights.

This takes us back to holdups and the assets at risk for each party. Zephyr might retain most decision rights about where Bob will be posted and for how long, because they are coordinating many different employees at many different sites. But, as already discussed, this leaves Bob open to a holdup. When, at the outset, the Zephyr recruiter told Bob about the job, she told him, "For a while, at least, you will be told what to do, where, and with whom." Bob was under no illusions about who would have these decision rights. So an important consideration for Bob was, "If I let Zephyr management control my work life to that extent, how much can I trust them not to take advantage of my situation?"

The issue of credibility becomes even more important when the decision-making party wants the other party to make investments in the relationship. Some of the assets that Bob has at risk in his relationship with Zephyr are created naturally, such as friendships with co-workers and loss of income and risk of a bad recommendation if he quits. But beyond these assets, he can choose whether to create more. Suppose, for instance, Alice asks Bob to attend evening classes, to learn Tamil, so he can better communicate with the local workers on the job. Bob knows that he can refuse this request; it goes beyond what he is expected to do, and it is his choice. Taking these courses will cost Bob some of his free time, and while speaking rudimentary Tamil might be an asset he can employ in another job, the odds are that it will not be that valuable to him except on this job or some other job in Southern India. If he suspects that Zephyr is going to use their decision rights to hold him up, he might think that he will get little return from an investment he would make in learning Tamil. Put the other way around, if Zephyr (and Alice) wants Bob to make this personal investment, they need to be credible in saying, "This will be good for us, and we'll make sure in the future that you are rewarded for undertaking this investment."

So what makes one party more credible? Formal contractual guarantees, including guaranteed appeals processes, help, of course. But, in this context, the third concept, *reputation*, often plays a decisive role.

Reputation—The Simple Story

Consider this line from the initial story of Bob taking the job with Zephyr: "He checked with folks who know the industry; they told him that Zephyr had a good reputation as an employer." This may have seemed a bit of a throwaway line when you first read it, but from the economics of this sort of relationship, it is in many ways the essential glue that holds everything together.

How did "folks who know the industry" come to the conclusion that Zephyr has a good reputation as an employer? Perhaps they had direct experience as an employee of Zephyr, perhaps (and perhaps more likely) they had friends or acquaintances who had worked or were working for Zephyr, who told them about how Zephyr treats its employees.

Of course, Zephyr knows that this sort of grapevine chatter goes on. They know that their general reputation as a good employer is valuable to them, both because a good reputation makes prospective employees like Bob-back-then more likely to accept a job offer, and a bad reputation leads current employees like Bob-today to be on the lookout for a better job (with a more reputable employer). Hence Zephyr will choose not to use its decision rights abusively. It will choose to behave as a good employer—even if abusing its decision rights will benefit it in today's interaction with today's employee—because not abusing its decision rights preserves and even burnishes its reputation as a good employer, while abusing its decision rights will sully that reputation, to Zephyr's longer-run detriment.

And Bob understands this. He understands that if promises

are made to him that are subsequently broken, Zephyr's reputation will suffer. He understands that this reputation is valuable to Zephyr. And, understanding these things, he can regard promises made to him by Zephyr as credible.

Reputation in the Real World

The simple story just told about how the desire to maintain a good reputation can provide credibility sounds great. But in the real world, relying on something as ephemeral as reputation comes with a lot of complications.

The complications start with the obvious question, *If Zephyr has the reputation of being a good employer, what exactly does that entail? How is "being a good employer" operationalized?*

In the real world, there is no exact answer to this question. Actions and decisions by you that affect your employees are many, varied, and complex, and they are often not binary but matters of degree. When Zephyr told Bob that he had to stay for another six months in Chennai, working for Alice, was this consistent with being "a good employer?" What about telling Bob that he was stuck with Alice in Chennai for another twelve months? If it were important to keep Bob in Chennai for nine months, and if a nine-month extension on the first year was longer than the norm, might there be some compensatory action that Zephyr could take on Bob's behalf that would restore Zephyr's good name, both in Bob's mind and in the minds of other employees that observed this particular bit of *What next?*

Common sense, experience, and what little theory we have

on such matters offer a few suggestions: First, to be effective, a reputation should, as much as possible, be based on bright lines rather than fuzzy boundaries. "We never do this" is generally a lot more effective as a reputation per se than is "We only do this five percent of the time." Of course, "never" is a long time, and you may have other and entirely valid reasons for violating a practice you usually follow when circumstances warrant. But you should understand that, if and when you do so, you are making it much harder for second and third parties to tell whether you are or are not living up to a reputation you wish to cultivate.

Second, to the extent possible, consistency in behavior, both through time and across employees, is nearly always a virtue in establishing a solid reputation. You can treat different groups differently, but you are more likely to be successful in doing so, in terms of maintaining a solid reputation, if there are clear social distinctions between the groups. (To give an obvious example, as associate dean of Stanford GSB, I could get away with treating the clerical staff differently from faculty members a lot more easily than I could get away with treating folks who teach accounting differently from how I treated marketing faculty members.) Next chapter, when we get to the psychology of employment relationships, the notion of social comparisons will be introduced: Individuals tend to evaluate how well they are being treated based not on some absolute standard but on their treatment relative to the treatment accorded to their social and work peers. This has profound implications for "consistency in behavior" when it comes to maintaining a reputation.

Third, bear in mind that in any action you take vis-à-vis a particular employee, you have two audiences: the specific employee with whom you are dealing; and all the other employees who are observing the incident. Recall in the story that Bob, aggrieved about being kept in Chennai and aware that if he quit, Zephyr would be worse off, thought of asking for a special bonus in compensation. In terms of keeping Bob happy, Zephyr might see this as a reasonable step to take. But Zephyr probably does not want, with all of its employees, a reputation for being willing to bargain over such bonuses. And even if they could strike a confidentiality deal with Bob—"You'll get your bonus, but you must never let anyone know about this"—do they want Bob to get the idea that, in his case at least, they are willing to engage in this sort of bargaining?

This point probably seems obvious to you as you read it. But my experience has been that, in the heat of dealing with a particular employee, it is too easy to forget about the larger implications for your reputation of the actions you take in the moment.

Finally, keep in mind that while Zephyr carries a general reputation for how it treats employees, frontline supervisors like Alice are making decisions that affect Zephyr's reputation daily. Of course, it is possible that Zephyr's reputation and Alice's are distinct, as in "Zephyr is generally a good place to work, but Alice is a real jerk." But, to be sure, if all your frontline supervisors act like jerks, your organization's reputation as an employer is going to suffer.

An important but, in my experience, under-appreciated quality in a good frontline supervisor or a middle manager in an organization is making decisions concerning subordinates that the organization wants them to make. This is, of course, another dimension of aligning the interests of the employee (in this case, the supervisor) and employer. Are you providing sufficient motivation for your frontline supervisors and middle managers along this dimension? Are they adequately educated about what sort of treatment they should be providing to the folks who work under their supervision? Are they adequately trained to be effective in providing that treatment? And, perhaps most importantly, are they making the right trade-offs in the heat of the moment? Alice, of course, has responsibility for getting her construction project done on time and on budget. If she views that as being overwhelmingly important to how Zephyr is evaluating her—and she might well have that view if it accurately reflects how she is evaluated—she might put less emphasis on keeping Bob and his peers content than, in the long run, top management of Zephyr would want.

Recap: The Economics of Enduring Employment Relationships

- **What next?** Enduring employment relationships evolve as time passes in ways that, initially, no one can anticipate or predict. At the outset, the parties involved know that they are entering into a "make it up as we go" relationship.
- **Assets at risk.** And, as time passes, the parties (increasingly) develop assets specific to the relationship. Walking away from the relationship means a loss of those assets; because these are "assets at risk," each side can hold up the other.
- **Governance.** In any enduring relationship of this sort, and in particular in enduring employment relationships, the governance provisions—specifying which party or parties, by formal agreement or custom, have the right to decide on *What next?*—therefore become crucial.

- **Efficiency, ability, and information.** Better decisions, more smoothly implemented, means more value for the parties to split and gives the relationship better odds of surviving. So, as a general rule, decision rights should be assigned to the party with the best information and the best ability.
- **Credibility.** But in addition, parties should be comfortable that they won't be held up or exploited by the decisions of others, and they should be willing to invest in the relationship (which means putting *even more* of their assets at risk). So, when assigning decision rights, the credibility of the decision-making party not to exploit that authority is important.
- **Reputation.** Perhaps the most important source of credibility is the decision-making party's desire to keep and even enhance its reputation for not exploiting its decision-making authority. Maintaining a good reputation is more art than science, but it is often the essential glue in the management of enduring employment relationships.

Motivation: This Framework versus Incentive Theory

Chapter 2 advanced the economic theory of incentives as the economic theory of motivation. And it is indeed *the* theory, in the sense that most economists, asked what economics has to say about motivation, would say incentive theory and only incentive theory.

When employing pay for performance as a practical motivational tool, incentive theory is certainly useful, in two different ways. In contexts where pay for performance makes practical sense, it teaches us what are the most important considerations to keep in mind when designing the exact details: Look for ways to eliminate randomness in outcomes that the employee can't control and that will frustrate him or her. When randomness cannot be eliminated, look for the most "accurate" measures of what the employee did (consider benchmarking and tournament schemes). Understand the need to provide the employee with insurance against random fluctuations in his income. Understand that schemes like this serve both a motivational and a screening function, for good or for bad. Think hard about the dynamic implications of such schemes, especially near the end of performance-evaluation periods. And the theory sheds a bright light on some ways in which pay for performance schemes can fail: Pay particular attention to multitasking issues and the way in which your incentive scheme "pushes" some tasks over others. Watch out for unanticipated and perverse effects of whatever scheme you put in place, especially one that is formulaic. And (on the other side) understand how subjective determination of rewards by supervisors can motivate activities designed to influence those supervisors, in ways that are rarely productive for your organization.

But, ultimately, incentive theory is based on a model of the relationship between employer and employee that is too limiting, especially in contexts where employment is an enduring relationship. Reconceptualizing employment in the terms developed in this chapter should alert you to the following considerations when it comes to motivating your employees that incentive theory, by and large, ignores.

- Incentive theory—and pay for performance, more generally—biases your thinking as an employer in the direction of measurable performance, and measurable performance usually involves measures of short-run performance. This is multitasking concerns on steroids: If your thinking is in terms of pay for performance, you may miss entirely the long-term implications of the scheme for the behavior of employees.

- Employees in a long-term employment relationship, in trying to understand what is expected of them and what they should expect in return, will naturally look at what has been expected and provided in the past. Your good reputation as an employer may be a very powerful asset, and your bad reputation, if you have a bad reputation, can be a terrible liability. And whether your reputation is good or bad, it constrains you; it is an object of inertia. You can't change it however you wish to suit today's dilemmas and issues; at the same time, actions you take today that will affect your reputation with an employee should be considered not only in terms of today's consequences but of the consequences for future dealings with this employee.

- And employees, in trying to understand what is expected of them and what they should expect in return, look at *more* than how you treat them, personally. A good case can be made that Artisans' Alliance from Chapter 1, by structuring compensation for its salespersons as it did, engaged in a textbook and entirely appropriate application of incentive theory, for the salespersons in isolation. But AA probably didn't give enough consideration to how this incentive scheme would affect the perceptions and therefore the motivation of the Explorers, who were the key to effective execution of the business strategy.

- The model of "governance" in incentive theory is that the employer says how the employee will be rewarded, and the employee responds within a well-understood and fixed set of "rules." Governance of real employment relationships is, of course, much more complex as events unfold to which you and your employees must respond; you should focus attention on the *process* by which decisions that affect your employees are made. This takes us back to the issue of how well your frontline supervisors are doing, as they make decisions in the name of your organization. Because I think this point is not generally given the attention it deserves, I reiterate: When you evaluate the performance of your supervisors, how much weight do you put on how well they do in "caring" for your organization's human capital (as embodied by your stock of employees) and in preserving your reputational capital with your employees, versus how well they do in getting today's job done?

- How an individual behaves vis-à-vis another party in a relationship depends on the nature of that relationship. How do your employees conceive of their relationship with your organization? Are they "just employees," or members of a team, or partners? How do you conceive of your relationship with them? Answering these questions takes us out of the realm of economics, as the discipline is usually defined,* and into the realm of social psychology. Employment is not only an economic relationship; it is, for most employees, an important part of their social identity and a source of social exchange. And the social nature of employment provides the employer with a host of challenges in and opportunities for motivating employees.

The pay-for-performance orientation of incentive theory pushes you away from thinking about the social nature of employment and those challenges and opportunities. The framework advanced in this chapter, while certainly more complex, accounts more fully for these factors, and points us toward lessons we can learn from cognitive and social psychology. So that is where we go next.

But, before going there, three grace notes are worth mentioning.

Employee Voice

A standard "principle" in business strategy is that your business will be better off the less powerful are your suppliers and customers. (This principle is enshrined, in particular, in the famous

---

* Although this is changing. In particular, I recommend most strongly a wonderful book by George Akerlof and Rachel Kranton, *Identity Economics: How Our Identities Shape Our Work, Wages, and Well-Being* (Princeton, NJ: Princeton University Press, 2010), which explores in economic terms how behavior can be affected by how an individual thinks of herself vis-à-vis those with whom she is dealing.

"Five Forces" of Michael Porter.[2]) But consider how Toyota treats its frontline suppliers: Toyota arranges for those suppliers to meet together at regular intervals; it provides the venue and pays for expenses incurred. Toyota does this for several reasons: First, Toyota wants its suppliers to educate each other, sharing best practices and, in particular, best practices in dealing with Toyota. If a new supplier is told by Toyota, "This is how we do things," it helps if the new supplier hears the same message (that is, "This is how you do things if you supply Toyota") from a long-time, successful supplier to Toyota. Second, Toyota can use this sort of forum to fine-tune its reputation with its suppliers, of being "tough, but fair." Toyota will, on occasion, insist on something with a specific supplier that may seem, to that supplier, more tough than fair. An aggrieved supplier can discuss the specifics at one of these meetings, with the other suppliers acting as a jury of peers: Typically, the peers will render a verdict of "Toyota is not guilty." And on the rare occasion that the verdict is "Toyota probably went too far," Toyota will know to back off.

A third reason for promoting this sort of meeting is that it makes Toyota's "promise" not to abuse individual suppliers more credible. It does this by *empowering* the suppliers collectively. If Toyota were to act abusively in its relationship with a single supplier, that supplier could quit the relationship, which would hurt Toyota a bit. But, because of these meetings, such abusive actions by Toyota would be noticed by all the suppliers at the forum. It would cause them (all the suppliers) to worry, "How will Toyota treat me?" It might incline those suppliers to look for contractual guarantees with Toyota, which would reduce Toyota's cherished and valuable flexibility. It might incline them against making sunk-cost investments in their relationship with Toyota, in fear of being held up by Toyota. In other words, Toyota, by promoting this sort of supplier forum, turns its reputation with each supplier into a reputation with all its suppliers. Toyota, in each individual, bilateral relationship, has its general reputation more at risk. Hence Toyota is more careful in its bilateral relationships; it has enhanced credibility in each of those relationships.

This is not always a good thing for Toyota. In some cases, Toyota might want to make an exception to its general policies with an individual supplier, an exception that would benefit both Toyota and the specific supplier. If it could do this "secretly," without its other suppliers knowing, it might do so. But since word of the exception is bound to come out, Toyota has to be careful not to make such exceptions, to preserve its reputation for doing business in a certain way.

What is the connection with the principle that you want weak suppliers and weak customers? If your relationship with your suppliers or your customers is based on your reputation, what keeps you "honest" or credible is the threat that suppliers or customers will hurt you if you don't act according to that reputation. If they can't hurt you (enough), they can't trust you. So, weakness per se is a disadvantage, if the nature of your relationship is one based on reputation-derived credibility.

In the context of employment relationships, this takes us to the issue of worker collectives such as labor unions. Ask the average American manager about dealing with an organized workforce, and the answer will, in most cases, be "Avoid that if at all possible." But empirical analysis of unionized versus non-unionized settings paints a more nuanced picture. For a variety of reasons, including the promotion of trust and more efficient assignment of decision rights, having an organized workforce *may* promote efficiency in the relationship between labor and management. In essence, it gives labor an efficiency-promoting voice in labor-management relations. But having an organized workforce also strengthens the bargaining power of labor. These two effects, *on average*, net out a bottom line for management that is worse with a union than without; labor uses its bargaining power to take a slice of the "pie" so large that management's smaller share of the larger pie with a union is less than its larger share of the smaller pie without.* But in cases where labor and management have a positive and constructive relationship, the enhanced efficiency can overcome the bargaining power; the enhanced size of the pie allows both parties to have more pie in absolute terms. The moral here is: As employer, your bottom line might improve with an organized labor force, *if* you take the time and trouble to promote a constructive relationship with the unions with which you must deal.†

---

* The assertion just made is empirical and, as an empirical finding, it is subject to much dispute. The original empirical work on this topic, which is the basis for my assertions, is found in Richard Freeman and James Medoff, *What Do Unions Do?* (New York: Basic Books, 1984).

† If this paragraph intrigues you, you can read more on this the subject in Chapter 6 of Baron and Kreps, *Strategic Human Resources: Frameworks for General Managers* (New York: Wiley, 1999). If you do, pay particular attention to the German system of labor-management codetermination, which separates the voice and the bargaining functions of an American union.

Does the "Gig Economy" Change Everything?

A lot is being written nowadays about the "gig economy." Instead of taking a traditional job, workers take short-term "gigs." There are a number of economic efficiencies in this sort of arrangement; potentially a better match of worker talents to job requirements; workers have greater flexibility in when they work and how much work they do; workers who can turn down jobs that don't appeal to them are generally happier with the jobs they do take. When the worker does her work using capital equipment (tools, a vehicle), she is more likely to take care of the capital if she owns it than if it is given to her by her employer (although there is nothing preventing a traditional employer from requiring employees to own their own tools and, in fact, this is somewhat standard in the building trades). Finally, there are legal and tax differences between the employer-employee relationship and the client–independent contractor relationship, differences that can make the latter more attractive.*

For a variety of reasons, the gig economy is growing. And gigs are, by definition, not the sort of long-term employment relationship that has been my focus in this chapter. Motivating independent contractors that are hired on a gig basis has some similarities to, but is not the same as, motivating long-term employees. It is impossible to say, generally, what the differences are because the details of how the various "gig markets" operate are important:

---

* And, in fact, state and the federal governments are "reclassifying" some client–independent contractor relationships as employer-employee relationships, in response.

Motivating, say, a heart surgeon who will perform a bypass operation (which is, of course, a gig) is different from motivating an independent contractor who takes jobs for a small handful of general contractors, which in turn is different from what motivates an Uber driver, and all three are different from what motivates an independent computer programmer who seeks projects from a website like Upwork. That said, the following points are pretty generally true.

1. The independent contractor working in the gig economy, if the gig economy functions well, is not as tied to the individual client as an employee is to his employer. The gig economy, if it functions well, comes closer to the world of supply equals demand than does traditional employment.

2. But the world of supply equals demand is based on (at least) three important conditions: (a) there must be a lot of suppliers and a lot of demanders, so competitive forces can work; (b) the thing—in this case, the service—being bought and sold should be a commodity; (c) the market must be made; someone or some institution must bring buyers and sellers together.

   These conditions are why I twice inserted the phrase "if the gig economy functions well" in my first point: (a) a tile setter who works as a subcontractor for one general contractor is a lot closer to employee-employer, and further from supply equals demand, than the computer programmer who puts her services up for sale at

Upwork; (b) there are quality dimensions to how well the job is done, and so some mechanism for transmitting reputations must be present (moreover, the nature of the job must be relatively clear from the start; "very Type-K" jobs are not good candidates for gigging); (c) an intermediary that makes the matches—and also helps with reputation transmission—is important. (Uber, for instance, is both an efficient intermediary—it has the information on both sides of the market needed to make efficient matches—and a trustworthy intermediary—it collects reviews on both clients and drivers. An Uber driver who accumulates a few bad reviews quickly becomes an ex-Uber-driver.)

3. The supplier's reputation plays a decisive role in the gig economy. Earlier in this chapter, I stressed the reputation of the employer. This isn't to say that the employee's reputation is unimportant; to the extent that decision rights are delegated to the employee, one wants the employee to have a reputation at stake, to protect the employer's interests. In the gig economy, this is even more true; indeed, a first-pass analysis of the gig economy would stress the worker's reputation, because in the gig economy, so many more decision rights are vested in the worker. It becomes critical how that reputation is formed and transmitted to prospective clients, and whether there is some third-party adjudication if the gig goes sour.

Relational Contracts: Implicit? Informal? Oral?

The picture of employment that is painted in this chapter is one of an open-ended relationship between employer and employee. Each side benefits from the open-ended nature, because it provides the parties with the ability to adapt flexibly to contingencies that arise. Each side has assets at risk—including their general reputations—so each side must, to some extent, trust the other side. But, the relationship works because each side is trustworthy: Both sides value the relationship and want it to persist and, importantly, each side values and so wants to preserve its reputation.

Various adjectives are used to describe this type of relationship or "contract." My preferred adjectives are *relational* and *reputational*, with particular emphasis on the notion that it is the values of the ongoing relationship and the parties' general reputations that, to varying degrees, are the glue that keeps both sides honest.

You may hear the adjective *implicit* used, as in *Zephyr has a variety of implicit contracts with employees such as Bob*. Insofar as *implicit* means *never explicitly discussed*, this is either a bad adjective or a bad idea. Even though Zephyr (and Bob) cannot explicitly specify exactly what Bob will be doing for Zephyr in every future contingency, Zephyr should want Bob to have a clear understanding of the process by which future contingencies will be met or, in other words, of the governance arrangement that comes with working for Zephyr. (And, of course, Zephyr should abide by that understanding.) Bob shouldn't be left to figure those things out on his own. Nor should he be surprised by changes in the process that he had no reason to anticipate. In my made-up story about the recruitment of Bob, I'd give bad marks to the recruiter for being vague about Bob's prospects for further schooling while an employee at Zephyr. Even if the recruiter can't give Bob a clear answer to whether this will happen, and there are good reasons to suppose that he cannot, he should at least be able to tell Bob who makes such decisions and how such cases have played out in the past. To avoid subsequent misunderstandings, in the first employment interview and thereafter, Zephyr should give Bob as good an understanding as it can concerning how things that are important to Bob will be done and decided.

What about *informal* or *oral* agreements? To the extent that the agreements are neither spelled out formally nor contractually guaranteed—think, for example, of Zephyr's oral communication to prospective employees about how it assigns engineers—these adjectives may be fully appropriate. But the relationship between Bob and Zephyr, and between you and your employees, will function better the more you strive for clarity and precision in what you can and do say. And, as your legal advisor will tell you, if you and an employee ever get to the point of a legal proceeding, judges and juries often hear only the word *agreement*, even if it is modified by the adjectives *informal* or *oral*.

5

The Psychology of Employment Relationships

Economics versus Psychology in the Context of Employment

The economic model of Bob's relationship with Zephyr developed last chapter is quite complex, involving ephemeral concepts such as *reputation* and terms of *governance*. But Bob's part—that is to say, the model of Bob's behavior—is relatively simple and straightforward. When confronted with the diktat that he spend another six months working for Alice, the story is that he calculates the costs and benefits of his two possible courses of action—staying with Zephyr or leaving—and chooses the better option. In general, in economic models, employees are meant to be doing this sort of calculation every time they have a decision to make; as an economist would put it, an employee calculates which action among those currently available is personally utility-maximizing and then does that.*

---

* In fact, in these sorts of economic models, it is worse than this suggests. Bob's evaluation of the benefits of staying with Zephyr involves the results of decisions he will be called upon to take later, so as he evaluates the current stay/leave decision, he must contingently

Not even the most rabidly doctrinaire economist believes that real-Bob makes decisions in this hyper-calculative fashion. Real-Bob might resort to making a list of categories of costs and benefits—and he might not go that far—but he won't do the sort of fine-grained calculations economic-Bob does within an economic model. The economic model's value is premised on the notion that real-Bobs act, more or less, *as if* they make choices in a hyper-calculative fashion, where the model is more valuable the more real-Bobs' actions conform to this as-if fantasy.

Psychology and, in particular for this context, social psychology, enters this picture in several ways:

- Psychology can help us understand what it is that employees value and why. Economists will pay lip service to the notion that employees value all sorts of things and then, for the most part, build models where the only thing that an employee cares about is his income.

- Psychology helps us to understand how employees evaluate their situation: What evidence are they likely to process and in what form? To what sorts of cognitive biases are they prone?

- And it helps us to understand ways in which employees sometimes systematically deviate from the as-if behavior assumed within an economic model of the situation.

---

analyze all the future decisions he will face if he remains and all the future decisions he will face if he leaves.

In short, psychology gives us a deeper, more nuanced understanding of how employees behave and why they behave as they do, where understanding the *why* then provides you, the employer, with more tools you can use in managing your relationship with your employees.

It is worth noting that, *in some ways*, these two perspectives on human behavior are complementary, not contradictory. Psychology provides us with a long list of things different employees may value, any one of which an economist *could* incorporate into the employee's utility function but which, for the most part, workaday economic models ignore. Roughly put, economists are methodologically agnostic about what people value—*de gustibus non est disputandum* ("there is no arguing about taste") is one of an economic methodologist's favorite Latin phrases—although for practical modeling purposes, the menu of things economists put into the employee's utility function is usually limited. Psychology complements economics on this point, pushing economists to build better models by incorporating more arguments in their actors' utility functions.

But there are points at which the two approaches fail to mesh: (1) Orthodox economics assumes the tastes of each individual are fixed and immutable; psychology is much more alive to the notion that an individual's desires can change and be changed. (2) Economics by and large imagines individuals with infallible information processing skills, who take into account *all* the information they have available. Psychology alerts us to biases and, importantly, to *which* information is likely to be salient to the individual trying to make sense of his or her environment.

And, in comparing the two disciplines and how they do business, there is this fundamental difference: While economists by and large work with one very general and all-purpose model of behavior, psychologists have multiple accounts of behavior that are much more dependent on context. My psychologist colleague Dale Miller has a wonderful way of putting this: "Economists like to show how seemingly different things are actually the same. Psychologists like to show how seemingly similar things are actually different."

So, when applying psychological concepts and frameworks, you must pick and choose those that, you think, are best suited to your situation and context. And with that understood, we can examine some of the concepts and models from psychology that help us understand and manage employment relationships.

Self-Perception and Work

To understand and predict an employee's behavior, a good place to begin—probably the best place to begin—is with the employee's overall perception of himself and the place that his job plays in that overall self-perception.

Without trying to be precise, self-perception concerns the individual's answer to the questions, *"Who are you?," "Who do you aspire to be?,"* and *"To what extent do you fall short of those aspirations?"* Answers to *"Who are you?"* can be given along several dimensions:

- **Personal traits.** For instance, "I am ambitious," or "I am lazy." "I am dependable," or "I can't be trusted to do what I promise to do."

- **Skills and capabilities.** What the individual believes he or she can do: This ranges from the general "I can solve complex problems," "I'm athletic," and "I'm an excellent communicator," to the very specific "I'm fluent in French" (if the respondent's first language is, say, English) and "I can write excellent code in R, Python, and Java."

- **Values.** What general principles the individual believes should guide his actions and, probably, those of others: "I believe in equal opportunity for all." "To each according to his needs, from each according to her abilities." "If someone contributes more, he or she deserves more."

- **Social identity.** In which social groups does the individual see himself a member? "I'm Buddhist." "I coach youth sports." "I am an economist." "I work in the trading department at Goldman Sachs."

The answers to *"Who do you aspire to be?"* are similarly dimensioned. And for *"To what extent do you fall short of those aspirations?,"* answers can range from, "I'm just where I want to be" (along a specific dimension) to "I fall short in the following ways . . ." And, of course, individuals can and will give compound answers: "I'm an ambitious blue-collar worker at Sun Hydraulics. In my spare time, I coach youth soccer, and I'm quite good at dealing with young boys who are just learning the game. But, most importantly, I'm the mother of my children and the wife of my husband: Family is everything to me."

Our self-perceptions are important because we try to live up to our perceptions of ourselves or, where we are less than satisfied with those perceptions, to our aspirations. We desire to exercise and exhibit competencies of which we are proud. We strive to behave in ways that, we believe, members of social groups to which we belong should act. We associate ourselves with groups whose actions conform to our values and disassociate from groups whose actions conflict with those values.

And, a feedback loop can exist here: When we behave in a manner that is inconsistent with how we perceive ourselves, we can dismiss what we did ("I made a one-time mistake"), we can invent situational excuses ("I did that because . . .") or, especially when we consistently behave in this fashion, we can reframe our self-perception.

Different aspects of one's self-perception can, in specific contexts, imply different behaviors. Imagine that the ambitious Sun Hydraulics employee, youth soccer coach, and mom must choose how to allocate her time between staying overtime to finish a rush order, making soccer practice with her team, and staying at home to care for a sick child. Of course, her choice depends on its consequences; if her assistant coach is fully capable of running this one practice, and if she can enlist another family member to care for the sick child, then perhaps she will stay and work overtime. But the importance of each aspect to her self-perception is also crucial. If "family is everything" to her, caring for the sick child is likely to be the choice she makes.

This probably seems obvious. But what may be less obvious is that self-perceptions, especially about social identity, can be *primed*: An individual's behavior can be significantly affected if, prior to the behavior taking place, the individual's connection to one group or another is emphasized to the individual. In the one study,[1] the authors primed a group of Asian women students prior to the students taking a math test: One-third were primed with material that emphasized their Asian identity; one-third were primed with material that emphasized their sex; and one-third were primed with material that was race and sex neutral. Conforming to stereotypes that Asians are good at math and women are not, the first third performed (on average) best on the subsequent test and the second third performed worst, with statistically significant differences. In a second study,[2] students were primed in one treatment to think of themselves as budding scholars and the other treatment as college "socialites." They were then asked their preferences between pairs of objects where, in each pair, one object had more appeal to a scholar and the second to a socialite. The choice behavior was affected in the obvious fashion and, moreover, the postchoice satisfaction of a subject could be decreased by *re*-priming the subject in the "other" direction.

Of course, an employee's work, the people with whom he works, and the organization for which he works all play an important role in the individual's perceptions of self. Put the other way around, the nature of the employee's connection to his job—where "job" here is meant to combine the work he does, his co-workers, and the organization for which he works—is influenced by his general perception of himself and the role his job plays in that self-perception.

A useful distinction in this respect is between *instrumental* connections to the job—where the job is a means toward some desired end—and *expressive* connections, where aspects of the job provide primitive value to the employee. The ultimate in an instrumental connection is expressed by the employee who says "I work for the money I'm paid. Pay me more than I'm currently making, and I'll quit my current job and work for you." Or consider Bob: To the extent that he is working with Zephyr to build his résumé, make some money, and see parts of the world he hasn't seen, all with the aim of someday going back to school and, say, getting an MBA, then his connection to the job is largely *instrumental*.

On the other end of the spectrum are expressive connections to:

- *Fellow employees*, if relations at work involve pleasurable social exchange;

- *An organization that shares the values of the employee*, as in: "I work for Doctors Without Borders because they share my values and my sense of purpose in life"; or

- *The work the employee does*. This can take several forms. Bob could take pleasure in exercising his skills as a civil engineer, tackling difficult construction projects. He might enjoy building on those skills. (Of course, if he wants to build his skills so he will be promoted or otherwise moved to a better job, this is more instrumental, as would be a desire to exercise his skills to gain the esteem of co-workers.) Or the work can be a "mission" for the employee; think of a pharmaceutical researcher, looking for drugs to help treat a particular form of cancer, or of a doctor working for Doctors Without Borders, or of employees at Artisans' Alliance, working to improve third-world economies.

As an employer, you should understand the nature of your employees' connections to their jobs, since this influences both what you can expect them to do and how they will respond to changes you might contemplate in what you do and how you do it. The story of Artisans' Alliance fits here: The Explorers were attached to AA because of the shared mission. Moreover, the atmosphere at AA, with everyone sharing in the mission, primed the individual employee to regard that mission as personally important. But, with that basis of attachment, the response of employees to top management's bringing in hired-gun sales reps was a predictable weakening of the attachment and a rethinking of why the employee was doing such a stellar job for less than market pay.

Four Organizations with Tight (but Sometimes Fragile) Connections

From the perspective of how employees are connected to their jobs at a particular organization, four types of organization are worth mentioning:

- A *mission-driven organization* is one where the primary attachment of most employees is to the mission the organization has set for itself. Artisans' Alliance is one good example; others are NASA in the 1960s, where the mission was to put a man on the moon by the end of the decade, and Doctors Without Borders.

- A *values-driven organization* is one where employees and management share a strong set of values and, typically, where the organization promotes each employee's ability to live according to those values. Ben & Jerry's, the ice cream manufacturer, was founded and run as a prototypical values-driven organization.

- In a *work-driven organization*, employees are connected to their jobs primarily through work that they find expressive. During its glory years, Hewlett-Packard allowed its engineers significant latitude in working on projects that they (the engineers) chose out of personal interest, with great success for H-P.

- In a *family-style organization*, the bond is between the employees of the organization, who form close social bonds with one another. The individual employee sees himself as part of a "family," responsible for and to the other members; doing one's job and doing it well is to some extent instrumental in providing for the "family's" well-being and to some extent expressive; each employee values the act of helping members of the "family." The obvious prototypes are true family businesses (unless the family is dysfunctional).

The term *psychological contract* is sometimes used to describe the relationship between these types of organizations and their employees: The individual employee has a strong expressive connection to the job, one that appeals strongly to a basic part of the individual's perceived self, as someone who is on a mission, who lives according to strongly held values, who expresses him/herself through the work they do, or who has a strong and obligation-filled bond with the other individuals who make up the organization.

Clearly, these sorts of connections can be very powerful, allowing the organization to "take advantage" of the employee, at least as long as the basic psychological contract is kept. But these powerful connections are especially fragile when circumstances arise that require breaking or modifying the psychological contract. For instance, NASA, as an organization, lost its mojo as the Apollo program wound down; the mission had been accomplished. In a competitive environment where product-line discipline became important, HP restricted its engineers' freedom and suffered similarly. As for Ben & Jerry's, when it was acquired by Unilever in 2000, major questions arose about whether the company would stay true to its values. The answers to those questions are in dispute: Accounts can be found about how Unilever was successful in preserving the values-driven nature of the organization as a division within Unilever and how, in fact, the B&J Division has "infected" other parts of Unilever with its hippie culture and values. And accounts can be found about how Unilever crushed the values that made B&J what it once was. Finally, family-style organizations can founder badly if and when the social-relations glue that holds them together is replaced by animus.

What Do Employees Value Most?

Of course, employees value the wages that they earn. But beyond wages they may also value many other things. A list of possibilities is provided in the box. That's a long list and you can probably think of other entries. The obvious question is, *For a given employee*, in a given situation, *which of these is most important or*

Things employees value beyond wages

- autonomy (the ability to determine what they do)
- power (the ability to determine what others do)
- status in the organization
- personal satisfaction from employing their skills
- satisfaction from exhibiting competence to others
- opportunities to learn new skills
- satisfaction from meeting goals they set
- opportunities to pursue socially worthwhile goals
- esteem of co-workers and praise
- friendships with co-workers
- satisfaction of returning favors to those who have done favors for them
- being part of a successful team
- belonging to an organization that shares one's own values
- having on-the-job relationships that conform to the local society's general norms concerning social relations

impactful? The extra emphasis on "in a given situation" deserves comment. Of course, different employees attach different value weights to these things. This goes back, at least in part, to the individual's self-perception and what is relatively more and less important in that perception.

But, in addition, for a given employee, the relative importance he attaches to different items on the list depends on how much of each he is receiving and how he assesses his position. Before the arrival of the salesperson mercenaries, Explorers at Artisans' Alliance probably put less weight on their pay than on their ability to pursue a worthwhile social goal, because their pay was adequate to their needs and pursuit of the social goal was very salient to them. But when AA hired the sales reps, gave them lavish expense accounts, and compensated them as it did, and as those sales reps interacted with the Explorers, the issue of compensation became a lot more salient to the Explorers. Or suppose that top management at AA decided to cut the pay of Explorers by 20%, explaining that the Explorers spent most of their time in the (relatively) cheap third world. That would probably make compensation a lot more salient, as would a change that made it difficult for Explorers to support their families (for instance, to send their children to good schools).

To shed some light on the relative motivational power of some of the items on this long list, I return to the surveys of Stanford Executive Program participants and MBA students. I asked each group to rate eight different categories of motivator in terms of the impact each had on motivating the respondent him/herself and the impact it had on motivating the respondent's direct reports

Table 5. Average Scores for Eight Categories of Motivator

		SEP participants		MBA students	
		average for self	average for direct reports	average for self	average for peers
Extrinsics	Benefits	3.90	4.27	3.50	4.08
	Pay	4.91	5.14	4.62	5.10
	Praise	4.99	5.17	5.24	5.09
	Job security	3.88	4.65	3.69	4.48
Intrinsics	Feeling good	5.45	5.08	5.39	4.94
	Learn & grow	5.55	5.04	5.66	4.98
	Acquire skills	5.05	4.86	5.12	4.75
	Worthwhile things	5.23	4.74	5.22	4.67

(for the SEP participants) or peers on their last job (for the MBA students).* The eight categories of motivator (in the order they were presented on the survey) are benefits, feeling good about oneself, the ability to learn and grow, pay, praise for a job well done, job security, the opportunity to acquire and practice skills, and the opportunity to do worthwhile things.

Results are provided in Table 5. For each group, the average or mean score given to the motivator is provided, which respondents were asked to assess on the following scale: no impact = 1; negligible impact = 2; limited impact = 3; moderate impact = 4; substantial impact = 5; powerful impact = 6; I [my direct reports/ my peers] live and die according to this motivator = 7.

---

* The basic idea of this survey, and in particular the eight specific categories of motivator, come from Chip Heath, "Lay Theories of Motivation Overemphasize Extrinsic Incentives," *Organizational Behavior and Human Decision Processes* 78 (1999), 25–62. In Heath's original study, he asked respondents to rank order the eight categories in terms of impact, rather than rating them on a given scale. But the conclusions he reaches are virtually identical to those I draw from my version of his work.

These data tell a number of interesting stories. Suppose we put the eight options into two buckets: four categories of motivator that are extrinsic (supplied by others)—benefits, job security, pay, and praise—and four that are intrinsic (related to inner feelings of satisfaction)—feeling good, learning and growing, acquiring and practicing skills, and doing worthwhile things. These buckets reveal two key observations. First, for the SEP participants, each of the intrinsics outaverages each of the extrinsics for themselves, and for the MBA students, only praise outscores some of the intrinsics. Second, for the SEP participants, the average score for "self" for each of the extrinsics is less than the score they give their direct reports. For the intrinsics, the reverse is true. The same pattern holds for the MBA students, with the exception of praise.*

Since the respondents give different (relative) answers to the impacts of the different categories on themselves versus their "others," the obvious question to ask is, *Are the respondents more accurate when assessing the impact on themselves or on their direct reports or peers?* If the assessments are more accurate for direct reports and peers, then the survey results suggest that pay and praise are most impactful. If they are more accurate for themselves, then the intrinsic categories have more impact, overall.

So which is it? Why do the respondents give such different results for themselves than for their direct reports or peers? It could be that both sets of assessments are accurate: The respondents are, after all, a self-selected group; the SEP participants

---

* Are these differences statistically significant? For the most part, they are; in many cases they are remarkably statistically significant. The appendix provides critical p-values for the differences.

chose to spend six weeks at an executive education program; the MBA students chose to leave work to go back to school. Maybe, on such grounds, the respondents are different from their direct reports or peers. Or perhaps the respondents are deluding themselves. After all, most people would prefer a self-image that emphasizes a "noble" desire to do good things and to learn and grow, rather than a self-image of being driven by "craven" desire for money, recognition, and so forth. A third possibility is that the respondents are mistaken about their direct reports and peers. Perhaps their direct reports and peers have similar motivations as do they, and they just assumed (or focused on) "the worst."

We have no way to know which of these are true and, in fact, I believe there is some truth to all three. But I believe that most managers underestimate the extent to which their employees and peers (and bosses) are motivated by the more intrinsic categories of motivator. So, as you look at the long list of "things that motivate people," don't be quick to think that money is everything or that it dominates the other items on the list.

Having said that, I caution you not to overprocess the data in Table 5, which present *average* ratings for the eight categories from fairly large populations. The answers provided by these populations exhibit a great deal of dispersion. I give some specific indications of this in the appendix, but suffice it to say that, within my samples of SEP participants and MBA students are substantial minorities for whom, based on their responses, money is indeed most important.

One reason why employers tend to overestimate the importance of pay is that they underestimate how much the "process" of work matters to employees; they tend to think of work as instrumental for their employees rather than expressive. The list should remind you that process matters. No better example of this can be offered than the general social norm of reciprocity.

Gift Exchange and the Norm of Reciprocity

The norm of reciprocity—that people feel obligated to reciprocate, doing good deeds for someone who earlier did favors for them—can be a particularly powerful tool for employers, when wielded well.

Consider Bob, asking for a transfer away from Chennai and Alice, as he hears from Jill in Personnel the bad news that Zephyr wants him to spend at least six months more on the project. How effective do you think each of the following three offers of compensation would be?

- Jill tells Bob that Zephyr wants to make amends, and asks Bob to suggest a one-time bonus amount that he thinks is fair compensation. Bob asks for $15,000 and, after some negotiation, Jill and Bob agree on $10,000.

- Jill tells Bob that Zephyr understands his unhappiness and, to make things right, is giving him a bonus of $10,000, partly as a reward for the good work he has done and partly to reward him for sacrificing his self-interest on Zephyr's behalf.

- Jill tells Bob that Zephyr understands his unhappiness, especially with the climate of Chennai, and is going to send him for a 10-day, all-expenses-paid, luxury holiday to Bora-Bora, including first-class airfare, which will cost Zephyr $10,000, a figure that Jill *does not* mention.

An economist would probably say that (a) there is no difference to Bob between the first and second scenarios—in each case he is getting $10,000—and (b) that both scenarios are better for Bob than the third, if Zephyr is willing to give him 10 days off, because he could buy the vacation package, and the cash gives him the opportunity to purchase whatever he most wants, or to save the money if that is his preference.*

A social psychologist would be less sure, saying that how Bob feels about these three depends on Bob, but that a case can be made that the third scenario will produce the best outcome for Zephyr, then the second, then the first. The argument is that in the third scenario, Zephyr is providing Bob with a personal gift, one that has been crafted specifically for him and, in particular, in response to his complaints about Chennai's climate. Bob, the story goes, is most likely to perceive this as a gift, which is then most likely to trigger the norm of reciprocity. In the first and second scenarios, this argument goes, Bob is more likely to perceive the money as compensation to which he is entitled and, comparing the first with the second scenario, if he has to negotiate the amount of money, that makes it even more likely to be perceived as something an entitlement.

---

* Obviously, there are tax implications to consider as well. But hold those aside.

Of course, the social psychologist is speculating on how Bob will perceive what he is getting, speculation that, depending on Bob, could be wrong. Had Bob majored in economics in college, in the third scenario he might well say "Just give me the money."

But, the idea here is that the norm of reciprocity depends on the initial "favor" being perceived as a favor or a gift and not an entitlement. Recognizing this, social psychologists sometimes refer to the norm of reciprocity as the process of *gift exchange*: You give me a gift, and I feel obligated to provide you with a reciprocal gift and feel fulfilled when I have done so.

It helps, psychologists believe, if the gift is personalized by the giver to the specific circumstances of the receiver. A vacation in Bora-Bora responds to Bob's personal situation, namely his unhappiness with the climate in Chennai. Indeed, even if Zephyr is unwilling to give Bob a bonus or a vacation (because, for instance, of the bad reputational precedent it might set), Jill might be able to make Bob feel better by showing a personal interest in his particular career aspirations: For instance, she could say that she has heard that Bob previously expressed an interest in someday going back to school, ask whether Bob continues to be interested in this and, if so, provide him with information about how that might be done. Just showing a personal interest in Bob and his future with the company could help.

Another quality that can affect the perception of gift or entitlement is the nominal source of what is being provided. The Men's Wearhouse—the chain of men's clothing stores long associated (in advertisements) with its founder George Zimmer growling "I guarantee it"—as a part of its HRM policies and practices, brought sales associates to retreats at a beachside locale south of

San Francisco. As part of the program of events, the associates were sent to San Francisco one night to enjoy themselves, provided with spending money called *Zimmer Bucks*. I doubt George Zimmer reached into his personal wallet to provide the Zimmer Bucks to the associates, and I doubt that any of the associates, cross-examined on where the money was coming from, would say "From GZ, personally, of course." But, psychologically, the extra spending cash was probably more effective as a gift because of its name; even if the sales associates knew that it wasn't coming from GZ personally, they still might think that Zimmer was personally responsible for its provision.[3]

Perception and Evaluation

Behavior is guided both by what the individual desires and by how the individual perceives her overall situation. This is apparent in the phenomenon of priming, where behavior is affected by how the individual perceives herself, and in gift exchange, where the perception of whether something received is an entitlement or a gift is a factor in determining whether the norm of reciprocity is triggered.

And in employment contexts, perceptions and evaluations are crucial to behavior. *"What is expected of me? What can I get away with? How well am I being treated? Does my employer share my values?"* These and many other questions, asked and answered by an employee, have substantial impact on what the employee does.

So, it is of interest to ask, *What does psychology tell us about what guides the perceptions and cognitive processes of employees?* The short answer is, *a lot*; more than can possibly be summarized here. But, from the perspective of employment relationships, the following observations are particularly important.

- **Psychological biases.** Employees are subject to perceptual and cognitive biases. They overprocess more recent events (recency bias), data that are particularly salient or available to them (availability bias), and data that confirm prior beliefs (confirmation bias).

- **Anchoring.** They anchor their assessments on the assessments and expectations of others. If they perceive that more is expected of them along a particular dimension, they tend to expect more of themselves and their peers (and deliver more). For instance, employees who are "trusted" are more likely (not certain!) to reciprocate that trust with trustworthiness. Employees subject to intrusive monitoring—say being frisked every day as they enter and leave the workplace—are more likely to believe it is okay to get away with whatever they can.*

- **Social comparisons.** Important on-the-job assessments concern how well the employee feels she is doing and how well she is being treated. And, in this respect,

---

* I asked several colleagues who are trained in social psychology: Could this be explained as an example of priming, in that the employee is being cued, perhaps nonverbally, to regard himself as a member of a trusted (or untrusted) group? Could it be viewed as an example of gift exchange, in which the employer offers the gift of trust, and the employee reciprocates by being trustworthy? My informal survey gathered all four patterns of yes/no responses, a testament to the quotation from Dale Miller offered earlier.

employees tend to rely not on absolute measures of these things but on how she has done and how well she is treated relative to peers she has on the job. An employee who makes $10,000 a month when her peers make $9,500 may feel better treated than if she makes $10,500 while her peers make $11,000. The technical term for this is *social comparisons*. And it is important to recognize that an employee engages most of all in social comparisons with those she *perceives* to be her peers, those who are similar to her demographically and culturally. Organizations can and do use this to their advantage: When they want to treat two groups of employees differently, they may deliberately enhance social distinctions between the groups. And they may employ availability bias here, by limiting contact between members of the two groups. When, in Chapter 6, we return to the story of Artisans' Alliance and what it might do to get over its bump in the road, the idea of creating social distinctions between members of the sales force and the other employees, to dull processes of social comparison, will be at the forefront.

- **Attribution theory:** When trying to make sense of the behavior of others, individuals *attribute* actions to personal characteristics of the second party and then predict that the second party will, in the future, act in accord with those characteristics. This is called *attribution theory* by psychologists. So, for instance, an employee of Artisans' Alliance, confronted by top management hiring hired-gun salespeople, could attribute this to "Top management feels that the mission is so important, that they are willing to deal with these interlopers." Or they could attribute it to "Top management has hired these folks because they (top management) are really after a big financial payoff." Clearly, top management wants to do all it can to encourage the first attribution instead of the second. Equally clearly, events suggest that top management didn't do enough.

- **Emotional reactions:** Emotional reactions to events are a part of human nature. They should not be over-processed but instead understood for what they are. (1) Don't discount the long-term impact that emotional outbursts, often quickly regretted, can have on co-workers. As the boss (or supervisor), you may need to calm troubled waters. (2) Recall the adage, "Just because he is paranoid doesn't mean that people aren't out to get him." You should distinguish between unfounded emotional reactions and those for which there is a basis in fact and, in the latter cases, deal with the reasons for the outburst.

Self-Perception Theory

Imagine that a co-worker of Bob—call him Bill—is failing in an assignment given to him (to Bill) by Alice. Imagine that Bob, who thinks Bill is an "okay guy" and who has the skills needed to assist Bill, works overtime to help Bill succeed, so that (in the end) Bill does succeed. Imagine that this cost Bob a lot of his free time.

Self-perception theory holds that, insofar as Bob instinctively lent a hand to Bill, Bob will apply attribution theory to himself, asking himself *ex post*, "Why did I do that?" Several explanations are possible:

- "I did it because it was an interesting problem that I enjoyed solving."

- "I did it because Bill is a very good friend, and I didn't want to see him getting in trouble with Alice."

- "I did it because, in the future, Bill will feel obligated to help me when and if I need help."

- "I did it because I expect Alice to notice and to reward me with a better fitness report, leading to a bigger year-end bonus for me."

And so forth. The point, according to the theory, is that, whatever explanation Bob offers to himself, this becomes a stronger piece of perception of himself, affecting his later behavior. If, say, he settles on the second explanation, then he is more likely later to go out of his way to help his (now perceived to be) very good friend Bill. If he settles on the fourth explanation, he is more likely to look for opportunities to impress Alice, to generate a bigger bonus.

We'll see in the next chapter how you, as an employer, can use self-perception to "mold" your employees in ways that improve their performance and how, if you are not careful in what motivational techniques you use, self-perception can mold your employees in adverse ways.

6

Psychological Theories of Motivation [1]

I f you ask an economist, *"What theories of employee motivation does your discipline provide?,"* the answer will almost certainly be the theory of incentives as related in Chapter 2. And, while there is no reason to restrict the rewards for good performance to money—indeed, a number of economics-based models focus on promotion as the reward for good performance—the formulation *pay* for performance will probably dominate what you hear.

If, instead, you ask a social psychologist the same question, you are likely to get a varied smorgasbord of theories, theories that are based in different psychological accounts of how employees think, what they think about, and what they value. This chapter provides a sample from this smorgasbord of theories. But, first, here is a story that knits together some of different dishes on the menu.

Beth Israel Hospital and Primary Nursing

From the mid-1970s until recently, one of the distinguishing features of Beth Israel Hospital (BI)* in Boston has been its adherence to the practice of primary nursing. Primary nursing was introduced in 1969 at the University of Minnesota Hospital and was first adopted on a wide-scale basis by Evanston Hospital (in Illinois) and by Beth Israel, around 1975.[2]

At Beth Israel, the impetus to adopt primary nursing came from Mitchell Rabkin, then CEO of Beth Israel, who was looking for ways to distinguish BI from its neighbors, most particularly Massachusetts General Hospital. Rabkin upgraded medical research at BI, but it was the adoption of primary nursing that was his biggest and most successful change, bringing acclaim to BI as a "patient-centered" hospital. Rabkin hired Joyce Clifford as nursing administrator for BI and gave her full backing to devise a system in which nurses would work *with* rather than *for* doctors. Rabkin, in an interview years later, said that he realized from the first day of his internship that nurses knew a lot more about specific cases than he did as a doctor, because they saw the patients much more than did the doctors, and he wanted to utilize the information.[3] Clifford, in turn, saw primary nursing as the vehicle to realizing Rabkin's objective and proceeded to implement this scheme.

The basic idea in primary nursing is simple: Each patient in

---

* Beth Israel merged with Deaconness Hospital in 1996, forming BIDMC, the Beth Israel Deaconness Medical Center. Notwithstanding this, to keep the narration simple, I will use the names "Beth Israel" and "BI" for this organization both before and after the merger.

the hospital is assigned a registered nurse (RN) as his or her primary nurse. Each RN who was senior enough to be a primary nurse would have this relation with a small handful of patients—perhaps three or four—at any time. A primary nurse was charged with gathering information from her* patients, to manage their care proactively, to advocate for them with doctors, and to be on call for the patient (if the patient had questions or if an emergency occurred) 24/7. When on a duty shift, a patient's primary nurse would perform many if not all the nursing functions required for her patients; she would brief associate nurses and be briefed by them concerning her patients when not on an active shift. With sufficient advanced warning that a patient would be admitted, the patient would meet with the nurse who would be assigned as primary nurse, much like a patient scheduled for a surgery would meet in advance the surgeon, the anesthesiologist, and so forth. To the greatest extent possible, if a patient returned to Beth Israel after an earlier stay, he or she would be assigned the same primary nurse as had been assigned the first time.

Contrasting systems of nursing include functional nursing and team nursing. Functional nursing is the most traditional and hierarchical system: Each floor or ward would have a chief nurse or nurse manager who assigned nurses to specific tasks and who was solely responsible for care decisions (to the extent that a nurse made decisions) and for reporting to the MDs. Team nursing is also hierarchical, with a so-called "team-leader nurse" for each team; decisions were made by the team leader in consultation with

---

* To keep the pronoun references clear in this story about Beth Israel, I use the somewhat sexist *she* and *her* for nurses, *he*, *his* and *him* for doctors, and *he or she* for patients. In addition, generic employees for this this chapter will be *she*.

her colleagues, and the team leader provided most information to the MDs. The major difference (as I understand it) is that in functional nursing, one or two nurses might be responsible for, say, bathing all the patients on a floor; in team nursing, the floor would have several teams, with each patient assigned to one team, whose team leader then assigned team members tasks for "their" patients.

When first implemented at Beth Israel, primary nursing was resisted by the MDs, who felt that it (a) eroded their status relative to the nursing staff, especially when the primary nurses approached them proactively with suggestions, and (b) complicated the process of getting information: They might have to speak with a different primary nurse for each of their patients, rather than speaking to one nurse manager for the entire floor or, at worst, a handful of team leaders.

However, the outcomes of primary nursing were very positive, which won over the doctors at Beth Israel:

- While doctors had to talk to more nurses to get information, the quality of information they received was far superior.

- Patient outcomes improved, because of that superior information and because the nurses were motivated to improve the level of care they provided.

- Costs were reduced to some extent, because of less duplication of efforts and procedures.

- Patient satisfaction was very high. In *The Service Edge*, Ron Zemke writes that Beth Israel gained "a well-earned reputation for putting an uncommon emphasis on patient care and service."

Also, turnover within the nursing staff was reduced—at a time where many hospitals had nursing vacancies, Beth Israel maintained a list of nurses from other hospitals seeking a job at BI—and standard job-satisfaction metrics for the nursing staff increased significantly. Rabkin had decided to implement primary nursing to take advantage of the information held by nurses about patients. He achieved this aim and, *at the same time*, motivated the senior RNs at Beth Israel to provide truly consummate effort, entirely without any form of incentive pay and in a manner that left them more satisfied with their jobs.

It is difficult, to say the least, to explain this motivational effect with the economic theory of incentives. Nursing is very much a Type-K job, and the economic theory of incentives suggests that, due to the multitasking nature of the nursing function, incentives for primary nurses, who must balance a variety of tasks, will be difficult. One can even make a good case on economic grounds that functional nursing, where individual nurses are given jobs with fewer and more consistent tasks, is the way to go. So, to explain why primary nursing worked so well in terms of motivation, we turn to theories of motivation grounded in cognitive and social psychology, to see if we can find explanations there.

We begin by reiterating that psychology, in comparison with economics and its one theory of incentives, provides a number of theories of motivation. This chapter provides brief accounts of some of the more prominent and useful of these theories. The list of theories of motivation provided here is not exhaustive; social psychology provides others. And, importantly, these theories are not exclusive; more than one can be applied to a particular situation. (As we'll see when it comes to Beth Israel and primary nursing, at least two of the theories I'll describe help us to understand why, motivationally, it was such a success.)

Often when more than one of these theories apply, they are complementary; they differ because they are based on different accounts of how and why people behave as they do and on different "psychological levers" you can employ. But they lead in the same direction; the prescriptions that one theory suggests will strengthen the impact of the prescriptions suggested by the other theories. (This is so, for instance, in the case of Beth Israel.) Sometimes they are simply orthogonal. Occasionally, they offer conflicting accounts and, more importantly, conflicting prescriptions.

This multiplicity of theories—further increased when you also fold in the economic theories drawn from Chapters 2 and 4—means that you, as practitioner, have the difficult job of sorting among them. That won't be easy, but (as I tell my MBA students when faced with a multiplicity of frameworks that might be applied to a specific situation) that's why you get the big bucks.

Expectancy Theory

In expectancy theory, the employee consciously considers three dimensions of every set of actions she might take:

- *Expectancy:* How likely it is that the specific actions will lead to results that she believes management wants.

- *Instrumentality:* How likely it is that fulfilling what she perceives to be management's desires will lead to rewards for herself.

- *Valence:* How much value she attaches to those rewards.

The theory predicts that an employee will choose actions that maximize her chances of receiving rewards that she values the most. Some versions of the theory make this prediction exact, by asserting that she computes the product of the two probabilities— the probability of achieving the results management desires times the probability that management will reward her for doing so—times a measure of her value for the prize. But, we don't need anything so formal or rigid. The theory asserts, essentially, that she takes actions that *she believes* are more likely to lead to *her perceptions* of management's desires, that *she believes* are more likely to be rewarded, and that provide rewards that are more valuable *to her.*

What are the managerial implications?

- I've emphasized *she believes, her perceptions,* and valuable *to her,* to emphasize that, from management's perspective, clarity is a paramount virtue: Clarity and transparency concerning what management desires, how management will judge the employee's performance, and what will be the rewards the employee will receive if she performs well, all enhance both expectancy and instrumentality, hence help to motivate desired behavior.

- Of course, the employee should believe that she is capable of achieving management's desired outcome, which presumably means that she should in fact be capable of doing so.

- And the rewards being offered should be rewards that the employee values. Hence, management should understand what she values. Insofar as employees (generally) value equity or otherwise engage in social comparisons, management should understand this and craft the rewards it offers accordingly.

Tracy Kidder's classic book, *The Soul of a New Machine*, provides an example of expectancy theory. This book, which everyone interested in management should read, concerns the development of a new minicomputer by a small group of engineers at a no-longer-existing company, Data General. The young engineers who were working on designing the new computer—designing both the hardware and the micro-code that would run it—worked very long hours in a basement in summer in Massachusetts, with an air-conditioning system that sometimes malfunctioned. They did this because they believed that this is what it would take to get the machine ready for market in the short window of time available (*expectancy*). They were convinced that this was what management wanted. They believed that if they succeeded in these terms, they would be allowed to work on yet another new machine (*instru-*

mentality); Kidder calls this "pinball effects." And they valued the opportunity to work on a new machine (*valence*). This all makes sense except perhaps for the last step: these engineers were willing to work extremely long hours in uncomfortable conditions for the opportunity to keep working extremely long hours in similar conditions. Why would they value that? The answer takes a complementary theory—self-perception theory—that is discussed later in this chapter.

Expectancy theory comes the closest of all the psychological theories to the economic theory of incentives: The employee consciously considers both management's goals and how management will regard observable outcomes, as well as the value to her of the rewards she will receive if she is successful. In the account offered by incentive theory, the employee makes these same "calculations." But incentive theory assumes that the employee understands flawlessly the terms of her "deal" with management, and is focused on the trade-off between efficient risk sharing and motivation. Expectancy theory is much more about whether and how well the employee perceives her situation, and how well the employer understands what the employee perceives and values.

Goal-setting Theory

According to goal-setting theory, employees are motivated to achieve goals that are set for them (by management or by themselves); this is a version of expectancy theory, *where the reward is achievement of a goal itself.*

Goal-setting theory asserts that, to be effective, the goal should be

- *Specific*, not vague.

- *Measurable*; the employee should know when she has achieved the goal, and she should be able to measure her progress to date in achieving the goal.

- *Achievable.* And the employee should perceive that she can achieve it.

- *Relevant* and legitimate. It should be perceived by her as something important to achieve.

- *Time-bound*, meaning that the employee can see from the start the proverbial "light at the end of the tunnel."

The literature refers to these conditions with the acronym SMART (Specific, Measurable, Achievable, Relevant, Time-bound): Goal-setting is an effective motivational tool when (and only when) the goal is SMART.

In addition, goals should be *somewhat* challenging: Achievability is part of SMART. But, on the other end of the spectrum, goals that require little if any effort to achieve provide no sense of accomplishment or satisfaction when achieved, and so provide little motivation.

While setting SMART and yet challenging goals may provide motivation, for Type-K jobs, many of the problems that arise in pay-for-performance schemes recur: When the employee's job involves several distinct tasks, do you set a single goal that encompasses all the tasks or a set of goals, one for each task? And, whichever you do, how does the employee allocate her time among them? Suppose you set different goals for different tasks. Since the reward is meant to be a sense of accomplishment or fulfillment, will the employee spend most of her time attending to those goals that give her the best chance of quick success? Or will the employee be more motivated to avoid failure on any of the goals? And what if achieving success in some tasks is intrinsically more satisfying for the employee than success in others? So perhaps a single goal that blends measurable accomplishments on different tasks is better. But, as in the discussion of multitasking in pay for performance, what if results in some tasks are easily measured while others are difficult to measure? And, since success in Type-K jobs often involves creativity, how do you simultaneously set goals that are specific, when the tasks to be done are ambiguous *ex ante*.

Imagine a job that incorporates two distinct types of tasks. In one type of task, the organization wants the employee to strive for brilliant success, even at the risk of failure, because the organization doesn't suffer much from the failures but feasts when an individual achieves great success. Such tasks are called *star tasks*. Think, for instance, of a researcher working for a pharmaceutical firm: Failing to find a new drug doesn't cost the organization very much in the grand scheme of things, but one breakthrough drug can mean huge profits for the firm. In the other sort of task, the objective is to avoid error or failure, because failure is tremendously costly to the organization. Such tasks are called *guardian tasks*: Think, for instance, of the captain of a tanker carrying a load of crude oil: Cutting a few hours off the time it takes her to deliver her cargo is marginally beneficial to the firm, but incurring a catastrophic spill is hugely costly to the firm; risking the second outcome to achieve the first is, from the perspective of the organization, a very bad bet.

The question is, *How do you set goals for an employee whose job mixes both types of tasks?* The satisfaction that comes from a brilliant success, if you set that as a goal, is tremendously motivating. Indeed, the psychological satisfaction that comes from brilliant success is probably such that no explicit goal must be set in that direction. In any case, the *achievability* part of SMART may be difficult to satisfy in such cases. And while avoiding failure is probably achievable, doing so probably packs a much smaller psychological wallop. For jobs that mix star and guardian tasks, goal setting will be difficult, to say the least.

Goal-setting can be a good and even powerful motivational tool *if* you can meet the requirements of SMART, plus challenge. But, especially for Type-K jobs, this can be hard to do.

Equity Theory

Equity theory starts with the idea that people, and employees in particular, have a natural desire to see that matters are arranged equitably or fairly. In the context of employees, the theory supposes that an employee looks at the contributions she makes to the organization and the rewards she receives, and compares the ratio of these two for herself to the same ratio for others in the organization, especially peers with whom social comparisons are natural. If the individual perceives that her ratio of rewards to contributions is markedly lower than the ratio for others, she is demotivated. She is also demotivated (or engages in some reframing—keep reading) if her ratio is markedly higher than the ratios of others. Indeed, the theory says that an employee can be demotivated whenever she sees inequitable ratios of rewards to contributions, even if it involves employees other than herself.

A textbook example of equity theory at work (certain to be featured in future textbooks) concerns Gravity Payments of Seattle. Founder, CEO, and majority shareholder Dan Price announced in April 2015 that he would raise the minimum salary earned by any employee of the company to $70,000 (taking three years to reach that level). As reported in the *New York Times*,[4] while reaction to the announcement was generally positive, a handful of the most productive employees were less than enthusiastic: The *Times* article reports that "Two of Mr. Price's most valued employees quit, spurred in part by their view that it was unfair to double the pay of some new hires while the longest-serving staff members got small or no raises." Employee Maisey McMaster is quoted, "He [Price] gave raises to people who have the least skills and are the least equipped to do the job, and the ones who were taking on the most didn't get much of a bump." She made her views known, was accused of being selfish and, already suffering from burnout, left the company. Dissatisfaction wasn't limited to the high earners: The article quotes another employee, on the lower end of the salary spectrum, as saying, "Now the people who were just clocking in and out were making the same as me . . . It shackles high performers to less motivated team members." And, a final quote: "Am I doing my job well enough to deserve this? . . . I didn't earn it."*

In equity theory, it is the perceptions of individuals about the ratios of rewards to contributions that matter. And, individuals have a lot of latitude in how they define and measure both rewards and contributions. This latitude can sometimes temper perceptions of unfairness. For instance, academic accountants are paid quite handsomely compared to their peers in other fields such as economics and marketing. But they do more or less the same work: They teach classes and do research. This certainly rankles economics and marketing faculty members, to some extent. But, at the same time, the belief takes hold—among both accounting faculty members and their peers in other fields—that teaching accounting is a particularly valuable and at the same time onerous duty. This raises the perception of the contributions provided by faculty members in accounting, and so brings the ratio of their rewards to their contributions somewhat into line.

And, when employees perceive injustice, instead of being *de*motivated they can be *mal*-motivated, taking actions like pilfering or padding expense accounts: Someone who perceives that she is unjustly under-compensated can respond by decreasing her contributions (which, essentially, is demotivation) or by (illegitimately) enhancing her rewards.

Because it is individual perceptions that matter, and because

---

* Since I wrote this account of Gravity Payments, allegations have been made about why Price decided to set the $70,000 minimum wage. See, for instance, Todd Bishop, "Gravity Payments Defends Business Practices Amid New Allegations of Financial Trickery," *Geekwire*, February 1, 2016. This is an ongoing story, and to see how it all ends, I can only suggest that the reader search the Web for the latest developments.

those perceptions are subjective, employers find, more often than not, that perceptions exacerbate rather than temper feelings of unfairness. Suppose that, in a particular organization, employees who are otherwise similar in terms of education, tenure, and other socially-relevant characteristics specialize in different tasks. To give an example, suppose Bob from Zephyr Corporation is primarily responsible for supervising teams of locals who are doing the actual construction, while Carl, who joined the firm at the same time as Bob, has been assigned by Alice to work at keeping the clients happy. It would not be unusual for Bob to perceive that, since he is involved in actual construction activities, his contributions are more important than those of Carl. Meanwhile, Carl is likely to perceive that anyone can direct work crews, but it takes deft political skills to keep clients happy; his contributions are more important and valuable. Now suppose that Alice has to determine annual bonuses to give to Bob and Carl based on their "contributions." Whatever she does, either Bob or Carl will perceive their ratio as below that of the other; if she gives them equal bonuses, they will both feel that way.

Another manifestation of this general phenomenon concerns the distinction between effort and accomplishments. Ann may be endowed with a level of skills greater than that of Bill, so that Ann can achieve a higher level of contribution (measured, say, by the quality and quantity of product produced) with a lower level of effort (measured, say, in terms of time spent working, for salaried employees). If you pay Ann and Bill the same, Ann will feel that her contributions are greater than Bill's, so she is under-rewarded. And, at the same time, Bill will feel that he is exerting himself more, so he is under-rewarded. Good luck with that one! Going back to the case of Gravity Payments, I bet that the reason the announcement met with generally positive reviews from employees (and perhaps did more good than harm) is that employees at the "base" of the compensation pyramid felt that they were working just as hard as their better-compensated fellow employees; perhaps the program provided the motivation to increase their contributions to the organization. The feelings of injustice quoted in newspaper accounts came from those employees who focused on (their perception of) accomplishments, not effort.

And good luck dealing with Ann and Bill if they are salespersons, and Ann sells more in a given period than does Bill, even though they work equal hours. Ann will perceive this as a matter of her skill; Bill is likely to think that Ann is "lucky" in the client base to which she was assigned.

Finally, and at the risk of going into too much detail on this one topic, consider the commonplace system of merit-based *raises* in base salary. Individuals who performed exceptionally well over the course of a given year get, say, a 10% raise in their base salary, good performers get a 6% raise, average performers get a 3% raise, and poor performers (who aren't fired) get only a 1% (nominal) raise. The problem with this is that it fixes base salaries for the next round of raises. Now imagine Ann and Bill are hired for the same job at the same time. Imagine they perform at the same level every year except for year 2 of their employment, when Ann does better than Bill. Then, while Ann and Bill get the same percentage raise in all years except year 2, Ann is paid more than Bill in every year after year 2 (and, in fact, gets a slightly larger dollar raise). Bill, looking at the ratio of his contributions to his salary, and comparing with the ratio for Ann, finds this entirely inequitable—Bill does just as much and as well for the organization, but Ann, year after year, is paid more.*

This all sounds terrible: Employees are demotivated by perceptions of injustice, and since perceptions are what matter, you, as employer, will have a hard time getting it "right." What do you do?

Psychology offers three suggestions. The first is based on the distinction between *distributional fairness (or justice)* and *procedural fairness*. What we've discussed so far is, in essence, distributional fairness: Never mind how it happened, the employee looks at her ratio of rewards to contributions and compares this to the ratio of other employees. Procedural fairness concerns the process by which rewards are determined: Is this process viewed (by employees) as basically fair and legitimate, even if it sometimes results in distributional injustice? If you can devise a process for determining rewards that is perceived to be procedurally fair and legitimate, and if you can focus the attention of employees on the process and away from the bare outcomes, this can temper feelings of distributional inequity. So, for instance, if your organization is one in which turnover is low and long-term employment is generally thought to be important to the organization, basing rewards on tenure—insofar as it is viewed as legitimate—can work well. (And, if you go down this route, you want to reinforce the legitimacy of tenure as a measure of contribution in other, perhaps symbolic ways: For instance, publicly recognize tenure anniversa-

---

* Stanford GSB employs merit-based raises and, from my decade as senior associate dean (with the job of listening to faculty colleagues complain about their salaries), I can assure you that this is no make-believe story. For more on the disadvantages of merit-raise systems, see Baron and Kreps, *Strategic Human Resources: Frameworks for General Managers* (New York: Wiley, 1999), pp. 258–61.

ries, with speeches about how important are the "pioneers" to the success of the business.)

One important aspect of perceptions of procedural fairness (or the lack of same) is transparency about the process by which rewards are determined. Imagine an organization that hands out, say, year-end bonuses, admonishing the recipients not to share what they are getting with their peers. Such admonitions may not be effective. And, even when they are effective, employees are likely to ask themselves, "What are they trying to hide?" This doesn't mean that you should necessarily publicize what each employee is receiving; for one thing, doing this focuses employee attention on the distribution of rewards. But if you have a process that (you believe, and you believe your employees will believe) is legitimate and fair, publicizing the process both is good in itself ("they aren't afraid to tell us how this is done") and focuses attention on the process and away from the specific distribution.

Second, you can try to affect the comparison set used by your employees to gauge equity. If you are rewarding different classes of employees differently, steps—real or symbolic—taken to distinguish members of one class from members of another can sometimes be effective. (When we get back to Artisans' Alliance, I provide some concrete examples of how this might be done.)

And, third, remember that rewards include financial compensation, but they can extend into other "goodies" that the organization can bestow. Keep the survey data from last chapter in mind in this context.

Self-Determination Theory

In the theories explored so far, motivation is tied to *external* stimulus of some sort or other: In expectancy theory, the employee consciously chooses behavior that (she perceives) is desired by the organization, so that she will receive from the organization a reward that she values. In goal-setting theory, while individuals can set their own goals, the sort of employment-context application I have in mind is where management sets goals for employees. In equity theory, the individual employee is reacting to rewards provided by and contributions provided for the organization.

Self-determination theory, in comparison, concerns motivation that is intrinsic to the individual. The individual acts in a particular way because she wants to do so, even absent external rewards or stimuli. The theory holds that an employee is more likely to be self-motivated the greater her

1. *autonomy*, the ability to control her own actions;

2. opportunities to gain and exhibit *competence*, to control the outcome and exhibit (if only to herself) her mastery of the situation;

3. ability to be socially *related* to others, to interact with, be connected to, and help others and be helped in turn; and

4. perceived *purpose*, the sense that the task achieves something important and valued.

So management, to enhance performance through intrinsic motivation, should increase employee autonomy, give employees greater opportunities to enhance their skills and demonstrate competence with those skills, increase a sense of "belonging" and "helping" others, recognize publicly when someone does well, and connect the individual's efforts to some larger and culturally legitimate goal.

And, to the extent that it is relevant, the employer should get out of the way of these motivating factors: Don't reduce autonomy, or opportunities for employees to gain and exhibit competence, and so forth. The most effective way to motivate employees is, in a lot of cases, removing *de*-motivating factors, so that intrinsic motivation can do its thing.

Given the problems in incentive systems that fit under the rubric of multitasking and other problems in getting externally applied incentives right, intrinsic motivation might seem like a motivational silver bullet when it can be enlisted: The employee does the right thing, all by herself.

Of course, it isn't that simple. Going back to the formulation of Chapter 1, motivation involves the alignment of your employees' interests with your own and then letting them use their own best judgment concerning what to do. This, then, is consistent with at least the first part of self-determination theory, that you should give employees autonomy.

But it is *incompletely* consistent. An employee who is intrinsically motivated is motivated to do those things for which she has a lot of intrinsic motivation—that's a tautology—which may or may not be the things that the organization desires her to do. If the employee's intrinsic motivation aligns with what the organization wants, it can be a proverbial silver bullet. But that's a mighty big *if*. The key to enlisting intrinsic motivation is to find ways and means to get the employee's intrinsically motivated behavior aligned with what the organization values.

And don't lose sight of qualities 2 through 4 on the self-determination list. These are qualities of "jobs" that (typically) give a positive jolt to an employee's self-motivation to contribute consummate effort to the job.

Self-Perception Theory

Self-perception theory was described last chapter. To reiterate, it is based on a process of retrospective justification leading to future behavior. The basic notion is that individuals often act without having clearly defined objectives; after the action is taken, the individual looks for a "story" that explains why she acted as she did, and the story she adopts affects her future behavior. If, for example, she justifies her efforts with the story that the work she did serves some social goal about which she cares, then her future behavior will reflect enhanced care about that social goal.

Recall the young engineers, designing the hardware and code for a new minicomputer in *The Soul of a New Machine*. Perhaps, at first, they worked long and onerous hours because of their enthusiasm for and excitement about a brand-new machine. But one might expect their initial enthusiasm and excitement to wane, as they continued to work under exhausting and stressful conditions. How did they rationalize to themselves why they were doing this? What kept them going? It wasn't some promised monetary reward; they weren't going to be paid a big bonus if they succeeded. At least as Kidder tells the story, they didn't have a lot of affection for the firm for which they worked. (They did, however, have affection for each other and the leadership of their group, and peer pressure could well have been involved.) They weren't engaged in any sort of social mission. All that is left to explain their efforts is that the work itself continued to be fun, interesting, and exciting. And, if they perceived this was what had motivated them in the past, it becomes a piece of their "identity"; they perceive that the work *is* fun, hence they desire to continue to have the opportunity to do it. Indeed, this process "manufactures" in them the desire to be able to continue to do this sort of work once the current computer is designed; if the reward for successfully working (under onerous and stressful conditions) on interesting and exciting work is the continued ability to do so—Kidder's so-called pinball effects—this fills in the missing piece (the valence piece) of the expectancy-theory story of their behavior.

Employees in some cases will have a choice of how they rationalize their past behavior and, depending on their choice, we get different values, and hence different behavior. Salience of a particular "story" makes it more likely to be the chosen rationale; to the extent that management wishes to employ self-perception theory to its own ends, it should determine which story is the one it wants employees to embrace, and it should set conditions to make that story the most salient.

For instance, in *The Soul of a New Machine*, Kidder

describes how the air-conditioning didn't always work in the basement in which the young engineers slave away, making their working conditions even more miserable. And the author, based on conversations with more senior members of the team, speculates that perhaps the boss of the team was sabotaging the air-conditioning system; the more miserable the working conditions, the more the team will band together in an us-against-the-world mentality, and the more they will decide that the *only* reason they are working under these conditions is because the work itself is interesting, exciting, and challenging.

Or, insofar as an organization wants employees to come to internalize the welfare of the organization—employees are willing to sacrifice their self-interests, at least to some extent, to help the organization succeed—the organization wants employees to embrace a story of "I did it for the organization, which I (therefore must, if this story is to make sense) value." An organizational culture that resembles a family, breaking down social distinctions when they exist, emphasizing benefits with special consideration given to those in particular need, and so forth, can make this specific process of self-perception more salient.

Or, where the organization wants employees to believe that they are willing to sacrifice themselves for some greater social good, making achievement of that social good more salient— think of a hospital that, in its communications with employees, emphasizes lives saved and patients cured and de-emphasizes costs saved—will help in making this the story the individual employee embraces.

Attribution, Social Comparisons, and Motivation

Self-perception theory is a special case of the more general psychological theory of *attribution*, described last chapter: When Cathy sees Don taking some action, Cathy wonders, "Why did Don do that?" The story Cathy tells herself is her attribution; and having attributed Don's behavior to some cause, she expects that cause to motivate Don in the future. Self-perception theory, then, is the special case where Cathy is looking at her own behavior, asking "Why did *I* do that?"

When people engage in social comparisons, attributions they make about the motivations of others can lead them to attribute similar motivations to third parties and, ultimately, to feed back into their own attributions. Taking this a step at a time: Suppose Cathy sees Don take some action, and attributes it to some underlying motivation acting on Don: "Don acted as he did because [say] he wants his team to succeed." She then expects the desire for team success to motivate Don in the future: "Here is something else that Don can do, which will help his team to succeed, even though it is personally costly for him. I expect him to do that, too."

But now suppose that Evelyn is someone very similar to Don in ways that Cathy perceives are relevant to motivation. Then, having attributed Don's actions to a desire to see his team succeed, she is apt to believe team success is also likely to motivate Evelyn. Put Cathy in a company in which she perceives *lots* of co-workers sacrificing self-interest to help their team succeed, and the inference that this motivates most people who work for this company can be very strong.

And now for the final step: *Cathy* works for this company. If she is socially similar to all those folks she perceives as motivated by this desire, she may attribute this desire as acting on her. And if she perceives that this is so, it will become so, at least to a greater extent.

Hence, if you want your employees to be motivated by this sort of desire (or by a desire to achieve some social goal, or to do whatever it takes to make partner), it is helpful to surround them with social peers who appear to be motivated by this desire. A consistent organizational culture around this type of motivation can be a powerful motivating tool.

Undermining: Do Extrinsic Rewards Drive Out Intrinsic Motivation?

The act of donating blood at a blood bank or during a blood drive is typically thought of as an altruistic social act. The donor receives nothing for her blood, except (perhaps) a cup of tea and a cookie or biscuit and, in some cases, access to the blood bank's supply if and when she needs a transfusion. Blood banks will play on this by "recognizing" donors; when you donate blood, you might get a little pin or sticker to wear, to exhibit your altruism. Blood drives conducted at the workplace are designed not only to lower the costs in time and transportation for this social act, but to give donors the opportunity to exhibit their altruism to their fellow workers. And, in blood drives, whether conducted at the workplace or more generally, the psychological rewards of being on a winning team are sometimes enlisted; the total donations by different work groups, or by all employees at a given firm or site, are compared with the total donations of other, similar groups, with recognition given to whichever group gives the most, second most, and so forth.

Despite all these practices, blood banks typically run short of what they consider is a safe buffer stock of serum and plasma. So, at one point in England, the National Health Service debated whether to enhance the incentives for giving blood by offering donors a token payment for their donation. Richard Titmuss, a leading public intellectual, successfully argued that doing so would be (at best) inefficient—any increase in blood donations would not be worth the expense incurred—and might be counterproductive; at worst, donation levels would decline. And even if donation levels did not decline overall, monetary incentives would discourage donations from individuals with higher-quality blood relative to donations from individuals with lower-quality blood (the latter being more motivated by the payments offered), diminishing the overall quality of blood donated. Titmuss's arguments proved persuasive (despite counterarguments from eminent economists Kenneth Arrow and Robert Solow), and the monetary incentives were not offered. In fact, and because of the arguments of Titmuss, the World Health Organization, as a matter of policy, encourages blood banks to solicit blood on a nonremunerated basis.

Titmuss's hypothesis was and is controversial.* But, if we sup-

---

* In part, the controversy exists because Titmuss offered little empirical evidence in support of his contentions. A relatively recent study gives some support to Titmuss's predictions; interestingly, they find that compensated donations diminished primarily among women, and there was no decrease in donations when subjects in their study are allowed to donate their payments to charity. C. Mellstrom and M. Johannesson, "Crowding Out in Blood Donation: Was Titmuss Right?," *Journal of the European Economic Association*, Vol. 4, 2008, 845–63.

pose it is true, what would explain why it is true? Three interlocking explanations are typically offered.

Insofar as donors give blood to demonstrate to their peers and co-workers that they were altruistic, the token payment might *undermine* this demonstration: Peers and co-workers could no longer tell whether the donation was driven by simple and noble altruism or by a (more craven) desire to make a little money.

Second, donating blood, before the payment was offered, was a purely social transaction. The payment turned it into a commercial transaction. Even absent external signaling effects, people behave differently in what they regard as social transactions from how they behave in commercial transactions. In other words, the addition of the token payment might *undermine* the donor's own sense of the social good she is doing by donating her blood.

Third (and very closely tied to the previous explanation), the monetary payment, even a token payment, may *undermine* otherwise virtuous self-perception. Imagine an employee who donates her blood for the first time during an on-the-job blood drive. She does so to "go along with the crowd." But, after the fact, she seeks to understand why she did this. She could tell herself that she did it because many of her co-workers were doing so, and she values the good opinion of her co-workers. Per self-perception theory, if this is the story she tells herself, her future actions will likely exhibit an enhanced concern for the good opinion of her co-workers. Or she could tell herself that she gave blood because it is a noble social act, and she cares about the welfare of strangers who draw on the supply of blood banks. If this is the story she tells herself, self-perception theory suggests that, in the future, she will be more likely to give blood, even outside the workplace setting of an organized blood drive, because she will come to care more for the welfare of those strangers. And this second explanation, if it causes her to give blood outside of her workplace, prompts a virtuous cycle: Giving blood outside of her workplace—and outside the view of co-workers—removes the "good regard of co-workers" explanation from consideration, and leaves her with (only) the "concern for needy strangers" explanation. So the more she gives blood by going to the blood bank, the more she relies on the "concern for needy strangers" story, which (the theory says) enhances her concern for needy strangers, which takes her back to the blood bank, month after month, and so forth.

But now add in the monetary payment. As she goes to give her monthly donation, perhaps she is surprised to be handed a token payment. Now she has another explanation available; she gives blood for the pocket change it provides. If she begins to process on that explanation, and if the payments are indeed token in size, she may decide that she doesn't need to sell her blood for such a small amount, ceasing her monthly trips to the blood bank. In a word, the token payments being offered to enhance blood donations *undermine* the intrinsic motivation some donors have for giving blood—more precisely, it undermines the reason they give themselves for why they give blood, which decreases their intrinsic motivation—and blood donations decrease, overall.

Psychologists have documented a number of situations—both field studies (that is, with "real-life" data) and controlled, in-the-lab experiments—which support these three accounts. This evidence rarely concerns workplace settings, so the practical importance of these ideas when it comes to workplace motivation remains controversial. Be that as it may, the following are the managerial implications:

1. For employees who have strong intrinsic motivation, loading on top explicit and especially contingent-on-performance monetary rewards can be counterproductive. This can be a matter of defeating virtuous self-perception: Giving the employee the possible explanation "I'm doing it for the money" could crowd out better (for you) explanations, such as "I'm doing it because it is interesting" or "I'm doing it because success of this organization is important to me" or, and especially for not-for-profit organizations, "... because the mission of the organization is important to me." It can be a matter of self-determination; the employee might perceive the contingent monetary rewards as an attempt to control her behavior, reducing autonomy. And, if the process for determining the rewards is unclear (and even if not), it could induce feelings of inequity.

2. And, when intrinsic motivation is strong and the job is Type-K, contingent rewards can undermine consummate performance. If you are rewarded for getting the job done regardless of the quality with which the job is done, you may lose motivation for going above and beyond just getting the job done. If the size of the reward is based on someone's subjective assessment of

how well the job was done, the subjectivity in that judgment can trigger a sense of unfairness in those who are judged not to have done "well enough," demotivating them altogether.

3. Both these prescriptions begin with the premise "when intrinsic motivation is strong." When it is weak, and particularly when job performance can be objectively measured, monetary rewards can do a great deal: This takes us back to Safelite Glass. But when intrinsic motivation is weak, you can choose monetary incentives or taking actions to strengthen intrinsic motivation or both. When you choose both, at least be aware that offering the monetary rewards may frustrate to some extent your efforts to strengthen intrinsic motivation.

In some contexts, monetary rewards are offered to jump-start virtuous behavior. An interesting (non-workplace) example is offered by economist Roland Fryer and his associates. They have run experiments in which they try to motivate inner-city school children to do better in their studies; the students receive financial rewards if they achieve a goal that is set in the experiment.[5] Some students were rewarded for grades, others for performance on interim progress tests, still others for reading books. In no case was there a statistically significant increase in performance for all students in one of the treatments; but, for one subpopulation, rewarding book-reading did lead to better grades. The authors offer several hypotheses to explain this, the first being (essentially) the instrumentality portion of expectancy theory: Rewards directly based on grades worked less well in improving grades than did rewards for reading books, because the students on their own were unclear on what to do to improve their grades.

Undermining enters the story as Fryer and his colleagues depart. How will the group that was rewarded for reading books behave, once they are no longer being paid to do so? One possibility, the "jump-start" story, is that they will have learned that reading leads to good grades and, motivated to get good grades, they will continue to read. But the darker possibility is that, through self-perception, they will have come to think that book-reading is an activity that is undertaken to get money, not for enjoyment and not to improve grades. In this darker possibility, once the payments cease, book reading by this group will decline to levels *below* those experienced prior to the offer of incentive pay.

So what happened? Fryer reports that when financial rewards for reading were removed, students who had been offered incentives to read continued to outperform control groups in terms of standardized tests, but by less than when the incentives were in effect.[6] This could reflect simple slow *regression to the mean*, or it could be that, indeed, students who had been given the incentive to read more, and who responded to those incentives, had learned how to enhance their achievement. Unhappily, data were not collected on the direct impact of their subsequent reading levels.

Beth Israel, Redux

How did primary nursing motivate the senior RNs who were placed in that role? The most obviously applicable of the theories just described is *self-determination theory*: Primary nursing provided the senior RNs greater autonomy and authority, it increased their ability to exhibit their competencies (to themselves and to others), it increased their level of social relatedness, and it enhanced their perceptions of purpose.

And one can enlist *self-perception theory*: A senior RN, awakened out of a sound sleep to deal with a situation involving one of "her" patients, or providing a service for one of "her" patients that a nurse as senior as she is would not otherwise deign to do, looks for reasons she would do it. More money can't be the explanation, since none is on offer. So what could it be? One possible explanation that works in either of the two described circumstances is, "I really care about the well-being of my patients." And, at least in the first circumstance, she could reason, "I enjoy being consulted and being able to use my superior knowledge of my patient's situation." There are, no doubt, other explanations that she could conjure, and all of them (at least, that I can think of) reinforce consummate effort on the job.

The story of Beth Israel and primary nursing, unhappily, doesn't end here. The Harvard Business School case study "Beth Israel Deaconess Medical Center: Coordinating Patient Care" picks up the story in 1999.[7] In the face of financial pressures, Beth Israel Hospital has merged with Deaconness Hospital to form Beth Israel Deaconness Medical Center (BIDMC). The nature of those financial pressures is acute: Both the government (through Medicare and Medicaid) and major insurance companies increasingly compensate the hospital based not on the specific services provided a given patient—so-called fee-for-service—but instead providing a fixed level of compensation based on the patient's diagnosis—called diagnosis-related group (DRG) compensation—or, even worse, a fixed fee per patient per year, so-called capitation. Primary nursing, as developed, motivated each primary nurse to advocate for "the very best care" that her patients might receive; Beth Israel must increasingly control what it spends on each patient, replacing "the very best" with "what is good enough in this case." In other words, the motivational silver bullet of primary nursing is no longer so silver, since it motivated behavior by the RNs that is increasingly misaligned with the interests of the hospital to control costs.

The case study explores how the new CEO of Beth Israel, David Dolins, tried to deal with the situation. I recommend the case heartily: Without going into the details, Dolins looked at a variety of possible programs, which ranged from "enabling" the RNs to trying to control them. In the end, he opted for a more controlling suite of policies—I suspect that he decided that it had become too difficult to realign their interests with the interests of the hospital—with unhappy but predictable results: He broke the powerful psychological contract that Beth Israel had with its senior RNs, leading to significant dissatisfaction and demotivation.

Did primary nursing survive? If you visit the website of BIDMC (in particular, that portion devoted to "careers in nursing"), it seems pretty clear that the answer is no. Based on what is reported there, it seems probable that a team-based approach is now used to organize the nursing function. That said, the website continues to put extraordinary emphasis on BIDMC as a patient-centered hospital; without knowing for sure, my guess is that if you need to be hospitalized while in Boston, BIDMC is probably a very good bet.

Artisans' Alliance, Redux

And concerning Artisans' Alliance, the psychological theories of motivation advanced here provide at least two and perhaps three explanations for what happened:

1. *Equity theory* applies very nicely. The under-compensated Explorers compared the ratio of their compensation to contributions with the same ratio for the sales reps and came to the obvious conclusion: It isn't fair. Either this demotivates them (that is, they decide to lower the level of their contributions, to get the ratios closer to equal) or they "increase" the numerator in these ratios for themselves, by attaching greater value to accomplishment of the mission. In instances I have seen from which this parable is constructed, the affected employees are much more likely to go down the path of demotivation.

2. In an environment where everyone was undercompensated and achievement of the "mission" was the overwhelmingly salient message, *attribution theory* (in the

form of: everyone seems to value the mission, and I'm like everyone, so I must do so as well) could well have been at work. The introduction of sales reps, who perhaps talked a little too much about their prospects for a big payday and spent a little too freely out of their expense accounts while visiting the Explorers, undermined this virtuous cycle of attributions.

3. And the decision by top management to hire "mercenaries" to represent the company to giant retailers—complete with a compensation scheme appropriate for mercenaries—may have led in-the-trenches Explorers to question what was motivating top management. This, in turn, could trigger feelings of inequity (equity theory again). It could lead to feelings that they were being exploited, hence, controlled by top management to perform tasks that were not aimed at a noble social goal (*self-determination theory* gone bad).

What might top management at AA do? If they had a time machine at their disposal, I'd recommend going back in time and looking for sales reps who bought into the mission, signified by a willingness to accept nonstandard and even subpar compensation packages. Absent a time machine—in other words, for real—I'd recommend trying very hard to break the chain of social comparisons. If it isn't too late (and it may well be), contract with a third-party firm to represent AA with giant retailers, a firm that in turn hires the sales reps. Or, perhaps, find ways and means to compensate the Explorers that indicate that they are different from the sales reps: For instance, offer them (the Explorers) shares of stock or stock options in AA, with a clear statement that this is for the "real" employees of the company—who will benefit financially in the same way as will top management—and not for the mercenary sales reps.

Stock Options As a Motivational Device, Redux

The suggestion just made—offer the Explorers stock options (or direct grants of stock)—would seem to run afoul of the discussion of stock options at the end of Chapter 2. From the perspective of incentive theory, nothing has changed: Most of the Explorers have little impact on the price of AA's equity (when and if AA successfully enters the equity markets), so this would seem to get the incentives versus risk-shielding trade-off all wrong. And, indeed, from the perspective of incentive theory, it does.

But, as a motivational tool, this still can make sense on psychological grounds. Prior to the ill-fortuned hiring of sales reps, AA motivated its employees through "the mission." The hiring practices of AA screened for new Explorers who, from the outset, were fired up about the mission of bringing help to the underdeveloped world. And, once hired, being in an organization where *everyone* seemed to be making a personal sacrifice for the mission only strengthened in each employee the perception that the mission was worth the personal sacrifice.

At this point, top management needs to execute a bit of a pivot, telling the Explorers, "Accomplishment of the mission is still important, but now, to accomplish the mission, this company must succeed. So you should—we all should—work for the success of AA." This is not an easy pivot to sell: Even if AA is successful, how much of an impact will they have on underdeveloped nations? In this particular context, AA might have a better shot at selling this pivot if it offers a piece of the pie to both the Explorers and their client-artisans.

The psychological story here is simple: Convince Explorers that they are more than employees of AA—convince them that they are owners of AA, who share in both the financial and social achievements of AA—and it may become easier for the Explorers to accept as a "necessary evil" the mercenaries.

In this case, giving the Explorers a piece of the pie—and denying such compensation to the sales reps—may have the effect of blunting social comparisons between the groups: "We (Explorers) are owners of Artisans' Alliance, while they (the sales reps) are just hired mercenaries." That's useful, in and of itself.

But even without this social-comparison effect, the belief in stock options as a motivational tool can be a simple matter of psychological reframing: moving employee social self-perceptions from the category of hired hands to the category of owners, which in turn can affect the attributions they make in a positive way. If there is a story that supports the common belief that stock options motivate in-the-trenches employees, it probably lies here.

Recap: Psychological Theories of Motivation

Expectancy theory: Motivation increases when expectancy (likelihood that certain actions lead to what management wants), instrumentality (likelihood that fulfilling management's desires will lead to rewards), and valence (likelihood that those rewards are valuable to the employee) are strong. Managerial implications: Set clear goals, with clear paths to achievement, and make sure the rewards for achieving those goals are salient and valuable to your employees.

Goal-setting theory: Achievement of a goal that is set is a motivating reward. Managerial implications: Set up goals that are SMART—specific, measurable, achievable, relevant, and time bound—plus somewhat challenging.

Equity theory: Employees are demotivated by perceptions of unfair treatment. Managerial implications: Perceptions of distributional equity may be hard to achieve. Aim for procedural fairness (which, in particular, puts an emphasis on transparency of the process, if not the results). Try to control invidious social comparisons. And look at the full spectrum of rewards you can provide.

Self-determination theory: Employees are motivated by autonomy, the ability to learn and exhibit skills, a sense of social relatedness, and a sense that work has a socially valuable purpose. Managerial implications: Enhance these characteristics in tasks and jobs, and remove barriers to feeling this way. (Of course, this takes us back to Chapter 1 and Robert Bass's principles of management.)

Self-perception theory: Employees, after the fact, look for reasons they did what they did. And the explanations they arrive at are strengthened motivations for future behavior. Managerial implications: To the extent you can, "steer" their reasons in directions that will align their interests with yours.

Attribution, social comparisons, and motivation: Cathy attributes motives to Don's behavior. If Don is socially similar to Evelyn, Cathy may attribute similar motives to Evelyn. And if Cathy is socially similar to Don and Evelyn, she may attribute similar motives to herself, guiding her future behavior. Managerial implication: Build an organizational culture where employees are similarly motivated, and a virtuous cycle will be created.

Undermining: For a variety of reasons that relate back to previous theories, providing extrinsic rewards can dull intrinsic motivation. Managerial implications: Particularly for highly intrinsically motivated employees, be careful (and perhaps simply avoid) piling on extrinsic rewards.

7

Motivation and Teams

The discussion so far has largely focused attention on the motivation of the individual employee. How does all (or any) of what we've said apply, when individual employees work within teams?

What Does the Team Do? How?

The term "team-based production" covers a wide range of possible activities, done in a variety of fashions. Once more, specifics matter: What the team is meant to do, as well as how, matters considerably to how the team can be effectively motivated. It is impractical to make a complete list of all the modes of team-based activity, but three very different base cases will illustrate why it matters what the team does and how.

Case 1. Individual tasks and team-based results. Imagine a situation in which Bob (from Zephyr Corporation) and his co-workers Carl and Dorothy are all involved in some project. Each of the three has his or her list of things to do, with no overlap. Each independently chooses how and how hard to work on his or her list of tasks. Their supervisor, Alice, cannot observe the work choices of the three, and the only outcome measure she can observe is the joint product of their individual choices and, perhaps, factors outside their control.

Case 2. Mixing individual tasks and helping others. In this story, we imagine that Bob, Carl, and Dorothy each have their own tasks to accomplish and, unlike in the first story, Alice has access to outcome measures for each individual. But, in addition to their individual tasks, each of the three has opportunities to help their peers. That is, Bob has opportunities to help Carl with his list of tasks, Dorothy has opportunities to help Bob, and so forth.

Case 3. Information sharing: brainstorming in a group. Compare this with a situation where Bob, Carl, and Dorothy are charged by Alice with the job of coming up with a plan for how to accomplish a particular task or, even, in identifying tasks that ought to be done to finish a project and then designing a work plan for doing those tasks. Instead of each toiling away on his or her assigned tasks individually, with (perhaps) the occasional helping effort of one of the others, the image now is that the three are seated in a conference room, trying to arrive at a consensus that can be reported to Alice.

Each of these stories is an example of team-based "production." Each can be the context for interesting insights into motivation and, more generally, the management of the team and its
individual members. But the insights are somewhat different. And
these three stories are chosen for their focus on different aspects
of effective teamwork. Real-life "teams" probably will be a mix of
the three stories in different proportions, and so in real-life appli-
cations, the insights to follow must be blended to suit the specific
situation.

Case 1: The Free-Rider Problem and Peer Pressure

We begin with Case 1: Bob, Carl, and Dorothy each have their
own list of assigned tasks. Alice, their supervisor, wishes to motivate each of them to work hard at their individual tasks. She wishes
to enlist economic incentives: Based on an outcome she observes,
she pays each a bonus. To keep the story simple, assume that the
measured outcome is the length of time it takes to finish the job,
where completion sooner is better, and so the bonus promised to
each is a decreasing function of the length of time the job takes.
By working harder, each of the three can shorten the completion
time of the job, which depends on the effort expended by each
and (perhaps) by factors outside the control of all three.

This is just like the basic story in the economic theory of
incentives for single employees, in that each employee must trade
off how hard to work against the better (on average) payoff he or

she will receive. And Alice may be facing the fundamental trade-off from Chapter 3: By increasing the scale of the bonus payment (and, presumably, decreasing fixed-income portions of the three's compensations), she increases their individual motivation to work hard, but she also triggers their risk aversion by subjecting a greater share of their income to factors outside their control, now including both "environmental factors" like the weather *and* uncertainty about how hard their peers will work.

Any of the complications from Chapter 3 can, potentially, affect this situation. In this context, *multitasking* issues are especially likely to come up: While Alice wants the job to be completed quickly, she is probably concerned as well that the trio do not do slipshod work or, in seeking to complete the job quickly, do so by exceeding their budget. For the moment, though, ignore these issues: Alice is interested simply in motivating the three to complete the job expeditiously.

It is here that the classic *free-rider problem* rears its ugly head. Bob, by expending more effort, can accelerate the time to completion, which improves the (expected) size of his bonus. And this also raises the expected size of the bonuses earned by Carl and Dorothy. So Bob, by expending more effort, provides goodies for all three employees. But Bob bears the cost of this effort alone, and if all he cares about are his own rewards and costs, he provides less effort than is "socially optimal" for his team; he free rides on the efforts of Carl and Dorothy, each of whom free rides on the efforts of the other two.

Of course, the amount of effort Bob chooses to provide depends on the consequences of that choice. And Alice, in setting the terms of the incentive scheme, can control those consequences to some extent. Imagine, for instance, that the time to completion depends on the three effort choices by the three employees only. That is, no uncertain and uncontrollable environmental factors enter. And suppose Alice knows (a) the three effort levels that she desires and (b) the amount of time the project will take—suppose it is 78 days—if each of the three chooses her desired effort level. Then she can (in economic terms) motivate the three by telling them, "If the project is finished in 78 days (or less), you each get to continue employment. If it takes any longer than that, you are all fired." As long as the desired levels of effort for each, combined with continued employment, is better than no effort and being fired, and as long as each of the three expects the other two to do what Alice desires, then for each of the three, the best effort choice is to comply.* There is still a free-rider problem here, because Bob's efforts are not only keeping him from being fired, but also keeping Carl and Dorothy safe. But Alice can overcome the free-rider problem (according to economic models of behavior, if conditions a and b hold) with a sufficiently well-designed incentive scheme. Indeed, even if there is some uncertain and uncon-

---

* Also, understand that, even in this case where no environmental uncertainty enters—where the completion time depends only on the effort level of each of the three—the incentive scheme "get it done on time or you are all fired" can have a dark side. Let's say Dorothy's level of effort can substitute for Bob's and Carl's—that is, if she works harder, they can slack off and still make the deadline set by Alice. If Bob and Carl are jerks, they can tell Dorothy, "We aren't going to work very hard, so it is up to you to make extraordinary efforts to keep us on schedule. And if you don't, you'll be fired along with the both of us."

For those who know the lingo, everyone working as hard as Alice wants is one Nash equilibrium, but it is only one of many Nash equilibria in this situation; this situation is essentially equivalent to a classic bargaining game, where parties have to decide what "demands" to make; if the sum of their demands are less than some fixed amount, each gets what he or she demanded; if their demands sum to more than this amount, everyone gets zero. And, as both theory and practical experience tell us, in such situations, a lot of outcomes—many involving the majority ganging up on a minority—are possible.

trollable factor involved, there are further conditions that would allow Alice to "solve" the free-rider problem by threatening each employee with dire consequences in some circumstances.*

Unhappily, those further conditions are quite unrealistic: Alice threatens the three with indescribably awful torture if the job takes so long that the likelihood that someone didn't do their part is close to 100%. For this to work, Alice's threat to inflict indescribably awful torture must be credible—something she can't do if the three retain the right to quit—and there must be some observable outcome that is virtually impossible if all three do their part. These are not (typically) real-life conditions. And, in fact, in real-life contexts, the free-rider problem is magnified the larger the team, since each individual shares rewards with more team members but continues to bear all the costs herself. When you get to the level where Team = Entire Organization, you have the story told in Chapter 2 for why, for most employees, stock options as a motivational tool make little economic sense.

In some cases, however, *peer pressure* can be enlisted: Going back to Bob, Carl, and Dorothy, we have supposed that Alice can't see how hard each individual works; she can only base their rewards on the results of their collective actions. But Bob, Carl, and Dorothy are, *perhaps*, working together, and each has a pretty good idea how hard their two peers are working. I've emphasized *perhaps* because this isn't necessarily so; it is, however, often the case that team members have this sort of information. If it is so, and if the three peers exchange social goods—they hang

---

* A classic paper in the economic theory of incentives (Bengt Holmstrom, "Moral Hazard in Teams," *The Bell Journal of Economics* 13 (1982) 324–340) develops this point.

out together, they enjoy each other's company, or perhaps each of them simply values nothing more than the good regard and respect of the other two—it's still likely that they might collectively decide that each one will put forward a decent amount of effort. This agreement is backed by the threat that if any one of them slacks off, the other two will withhold the camaraderie that each one enjoys or will simply think less of the slacker, in case each values the respect of the other two. As long as the value of camaraderie (relative to its loss) exceeds the individualistic benefits of slacking off, each team member, on a purely selfish basis, will put forward the team-determined level of effort, to the benefit of all.

When it comes to peer pressure, the size and social composition of the team and, in particular, its level of social homogeneity play an important role: Both the level of social goods exchanged by team members and the team's cohesion in denying those goods to team members who do not conform to performance norms is probably more likely to be present in a smaller and socially homogeneous team. This is not to say that creating socially diverse teams is a bad idea; other factors besides enabling peer pressure favor more diverse teams; we'll see some of them later in this chapter. But to the extent that your organization relies on peer pressure to enforce performance norms within teams, the returns from team-bonding activities are usually high for teams that are demographically diverse.

Keep in mind, though, that peer pressure is not always your friend. In some industrial settings, peer pressure is exerted by work groups to *hold back* effort levels; those who outperform their peers are shunned as rate-busters or worse, especially in settings where rate-busting performances are used by management to hold the feet of other employees to the proverbial fire. If the team or group ethos is that its collective interests are aligned with those of the larger organization, peer pressure within the team can be a good thing for the organization. If the team views itself as being in an adversarial relationship with the rest of the organization, peer pressure can be a negative.

Also on this point, extremely close-knit teams that see themselves in an adversarial relationship with the organization can protect weaker-performing members of the team out of loyalty to one another. Especially where a weak performance by any one employee can have very bad consequences for the organization as a whole—think of the crew of an oil tanker, working on different tasks to prevent oil spills, where the cause of spill when and if it happens is not easily traced back to which member of the crew screwed up—this can have terrible consequences for the organization.

And, finally, reliance on peer pressure can present a different sort of problem, as hinted at in the first footnote of this chapter. Suppose the workgroup has cliques. To take a common situation, suppose Bob and Dorothy have worked together on many projects, while Carl is new to the company. Bob and Dorothy might band together, to pressure Carl to work extremely hard while they coast. If Carl can look forward to a time when he'll be an accepted member of the top-dog group, we might be okay with this sort of pattern of behavior, using terms like "rites of passage." But if you are building a socially, ethnically, or racially diverse workgroup, you had better be alive to the possibility that one of the "outs" may never do enough to become an "in."

Psychological Theories of Motivation and the Free-Rider Problem

The free-rider problem is minimized when "psychological goods" are the mechanism for aligning interests. Take goal-setting theory, for instance, where the achievement of a goal is a motivating reward (if the goal is SMART). The satisfaction that a team member takes from achievement of a goal is not obviously diminished by the fact that other team members share in that satisfaction. To some extent, this depends on the psychology of the group; in a close-knit and cohesive team, team members might get more satisfaction from a team-based achievement, but in a contentious team, the reverse might be true. ("I'm sharing my success with those idiots on my team.")

Similarly, the intrinsic enjoyment taken from accomplishing an interesting or exciting team project isn't directly diminished by sharing the interest or excitement with others. And the satisfaction of helping the larger organization to succeed is similarly undiminished. Indeed, insofar as working in a team, as a team, leads team members to enjoy the social connections team membership provides (per self-determination theory) and to internalize the welfare of their teammates (per self-perception theory), even where incentives are tangible and split among teammates, the free-rider phenomenon shrinks.

On the other hand, the application of equity theory to team-based rewards and work can raise motivational issues: If members of a team prospectively share in the rewards, whether tangible or more psychological, and if some members of the team feel that other members are not doing their fair share, the first group may be demotivated by feelings of distributive inequity.

That said, and with the proviso that the specific circumstances matter a lot, the case for psychologically based motivation instead of economic incentives is strengthened for team-based work relative to individual-based work. In contexts where economic incentives are the better option for motivating *individuals*, psychologically based motivation may well be the better option for motivating effective teams. And where psychologically based motivation is more effective for the individual, it is likely to have an even larger advantage for well-constructed teams.

Case 2: Motivating Help

Let's turn next to Case 2, the common situation in which each individual's job mixes his own list of tasks with opportunities to help other individuals. This is, of course, a multitasking issue, and the big questions are, *Should you (as employer) provide explicit incentives to motivate the employee to help his fellows?* and *Should you dial down the explicit incentives for individual tasks, so as not to remove the motivation to help others?*

As we now know, the difficulty with any multitasking issue is getting the right balance with formula-based economic incentives. But, because multitasking here involves doing your own thing but also helping others with their tasks when you can, in some cases you have a new and potentially powerful tool on which you can depend: *reciprocal cooperation*. Imagine a situation in which members of a group of employees—preferably a small and cohesive group—can extend helpful efforts to one another. If each individual in the group is motivated to achieve his or her own goals, each may be "organically" motivated to help others, in return for which the individual can reasonably expect help when he needs it. Put Bob, Carl, and Dorothy in a situation where each can help the others on occasion, and keep them in that situation. Then each, in his or her own best (private) interests, can come to see the logic of extending help in order to receive help.

Two caveats concerning "emergent" cooperation based on reciprocity are worth noting explicitly. Both are based on the observation that Bob will help Carl, based on reciprocity, if Bob expects that Carl will (a) have the opportunity to reciprocate and (b) will take that opportunity to reciprocate.

- If Carl's opportunities to help Bob are very rare, the first condition may not be met. Ideally, where helping efforts are important, you should try to keep groups small to increase the occurrence of helping opportunities. And if that isn't possible? Imagine, for instance, that the work group is large, and each member of the group sees opportunities to help other members, but bilateral opportunities (where Bob can help Carl and, soon thereafter, Carl can help Bob) are infrequent. In such circumstances, you should try first to promote a culture in which, when Bob helps Carl, he is not helping Carl specifically but instead the entire workgroup and, second, you should promote the idea that when Bob helps Carl, Carl acknowledges this publicly, so that all members of the workgroup understand that Bob is "due" some reciprocal help from whichever member of the group has the opportunity to provide it. Think, for instance, of the common practice of goal scorers in soccer pointing publicly to teammates whose actions were instrumental in creating the goal. Of course, this sharing of glory motivates the helpful teammate to be helpful in the future and, perhaps, this is the chief effect. But it also acknowledges to teammates that "my teammate just did me a solid, and it is up to all of us to take opportunities to do the same for him or her."

- A common situation where helping efforts are important is where more experienced employees are called upon to help less experienced employees "learn the ropes" or "come up to speed." At an extreme, a workgroup may have a lead employee whose job description includes taking time to help newer members. In such cases, lead employee Alex may have many opportunities to help new employee Barbara, while Barbara has few if any opportunities to help Alex. Expectations that Alex will help Barbara based on calculations of reciprocity are unlikely to bear fruit; you will probably need to find other ways to reward Alex for doing so. And, in situations where another part of Alex's job involves pay-for-performance compensation for Alex's own tasks, you may need to dial down Alex's incentives for his own tasks, so that you don't crowd out his efforts to help others.

Parceling Out Tasks

So far, we've been thinking about teams whose individual contributions on individually assigned tasks lead to a single team-based outcome. That is, Bob, Carl, and Dorothy take on different tasks that each does individually. Bob might design and manage the construction of some infrastructure; Dorothy, meanwhile, takes care of procurement of materials; and Carl manages relationships with the client. Each piece of what the team does is clear; the different pieces are parceled out to the members of the team, each of whom then goes off to accomplish his or her assignment, perhaps getting assistance from other members of the team, but this is help provided concerning the individual's assigned task.

In this image of how the team operates, a natural question is, *How are the different tasks assigned or parceled out?* Where the team consists of specialists, each specialist uniquely qualified for his or her task, assignment based on skills and specializations is natural. Think, for instance, of a surgical team; it is pretty clear that the anesthesiologist should handle anesthetizing the patient, not making incisions, and so forth.

But what if the team is made up of generalists, each of whom could take on many of the individual tasks? What if Bob, Dorothy, and Carl are all young civil engineers? If Carl, say, is particularly talented at client relationships, should he "specialize" in this part of the overall job? How does this affect his prospects? Should Bob be given a turn with the clients, so that (a) he can learn by doing and (b) his skill at this part of the job can be evaluated by the organization? And, more in the nature of process, should the team be allowed to organize itself, in the sense that the team members meet and divide up what must be done? Or should management—that is, Alice—tell each team member which pieces of the overall job to do? Motivationally, allowing the team to organize itself probably has advantages in terms of autonomy; countervailing factors are whether the team is sufficiently cohesive so that no team member is taken advantage of by a less-than-friendly majority and (perhaps!) whether the team's perspective properly balances the long- and short-run consequences of their actions. The parenthetical "perhaps!" is there because this is a consideration that can go either way: Bob may be more concerned with building his skill set for the long run than is Alice, if all Alice is interested in (is motivated to do) is to get the immediate job done as well as possible.

Bottom line? Like virtually everything else in this book, it depends. Each scheme—top-down assignment or self-organization—has its good points and its bad, and it is up to you to decide which works better in your situation. But, I suggest that you should be particularly sensitive to two things: First, consistency of practice is a virtue; allowing self-organization in some cases and top-down assignment of tasks in others, based on specific issues in specific cases, can breed feelings of unfair treatment. Second, whether you choose top-down assignment or self-organization, keep in mind the long-term implications for the development of team members' skill sets. If you choose top-down assignment, and even more if you leave the assignment to a supervisor like Alice, getting the job done quickly and efficiently can take precedence over giving team members the opportunity to develop. And if you rely on self-organization, team members who feel (perhaps justly) that they will be judged on how well they do in today's task, or who look for the most immediately convenient assignment scheme, will also favor short-run expediency over longer-term skills development.

Case 3: Teams That Brainstorm

And what if the team members' activities involve more intensely collaborative work? Suppose, for instance, the team is assembled to brainstorm solutions to some given problem or even to identify problems or opportunities to be addressed.

This is the sort of situation for which diversity of team membership is widely celebrated: A group whose members are diverse in terms of backgrounds, experiences, and talents is, it is commonly held, more likely to discover good ideas and to see the flaws in less good ideas than is a group whose members are similar in terms of outlook and training.

But especially in these sorts of teams, interpersonal dynamics are crucial. To give just a flavor of the issues that arise (and to pick out an issue that is tied to motivation): When the team emerges with a "solution," it is natural for the boss to ask, "Who came up with that idea?" (I'm assuming that the solution was well received by the boss, here. The question "Who came up with that idea?" can be asked with a number of different inflections, motivating vastly different responses.) Of course, you (as boss) want to know which of your team members are creative or have good ideas. But keep in mind that this practice motivates team members to argue for their answer, even if (in their heart of hearts) they know that someone else has a better answer. Moreover, the generation of a good idea in a group is the product of more than someone coming up with the final "answer." It could well be that a different member of the group, early in the group meeting, asked a crucial question that led the group to the point where the final answer emerged.*

And even if everyone on a team has interests that are well aligned with the organization's interests, they naturally have other interests that can interfere. Even if the boss avoids assigning "credit" to individual team members based on who seems to have authored the group solution, the personal pride and status within the group that comes from seeing your idea emerge as the winner can still push people to argue too long and too hard.†

This issue—the motivation to "win" in a team-based decision process—is only one of many issues that arise in managing a team that is asked to come (creatively) to a decision, issues that go well beyond motivation. Entire books—good books—have been written on this topic; and this is not the place to launch into an entirely different book. So I'll say the obvious: Laissez-faire management of this sort of team—that is, put them in a room and let them sort it out—is undoubtedly a bad idea. For an introduction

---

* Two cheap, but not necessarily trivial, "process" suggestions about this are: (1) Don't ask, "Who came up with that idea?" Instead ask, "How did the group arrive at that answer?" and (2) Encourage the soccer practice of honor-sharing. Encourage a culture in which Ann, if she is identified as the author of the idea, points out whose contributions inspired her, and so forth.

† When I teach a case study in courses, I often take advantage of this phenomenon by asking students to vote, before our discussion, on which course of action they think is right for that particular case. In a case discussion, I'm trying to get the students to explore all the options, and getting them "committed" up front to a particular answer ensures that, even if one option is a loser, its death in conversation will take place only after all its flaws (and virtues) have been hashed out.

to some of the better ideas, I'll leave you with a couple of recommendations for learning about the creation and management of this sort (and other sorts) of teams: *Making the Team*, 5th Edition (Boston: Pearson, 2013) by Leigh Thompson; and *Collaborative Intelligence: Using Teams to Solve Hard Problems* (San Francisco: Berrett-Koehler, 2011) by J. Richard Hackman.

Recap: Motivating Teams

1. **One size does not fit all.** Team motivation depends entirely on what the team is being asked to do, as a team. "One size fits all" is almost never true when it comes to motivation; team motivation is a domain in which "one size fits all" doesn't even make sense.

2. **Beware the free rider.** When the issue is that measures of individual performance are lacking, so any contingent rewards must be based on joint-performance measures, the free-rider problem arises. Peer pressure within the team can be a manager's friend in such cases, but watch out for peer pressure that works against management's interests.

3. **Rely on psychological rewards.** Psychological rewards rather than pay-for-(team)-performance rewards are generally advantageous in these settings, because they need not be "divided" among team members.

4. **Boost reciprocal cooperation.** When the issue is having team members assist one another with their privately assigned tasks, look to engage reciprocal cooperation that emerges "organically," rather than trying to "make cooperation happen" by imposing a reward scheme.

5. **Manage the brainstorm.** And when it comes to teams that are tasked with collectively arriving at a good solution, management of the team process is important; time to add to your list of things to read.

8

Motivation and Your Organization

Perhaps you picked up this book in the hope that it would provide an easy, specific plan to improve the motivation of employees at your organization. As I said at the start, I can't provide any concrete and definite recommendations how you might do this, because such recommendations necessarily depend on a host of specifics about your organization that I don't know. Instead, what I've tried to do is to give you some tools for thinking about motivation, in the hope that those tools, combined with your understanding of your own situation, will lead you to better motivation.

I've used the word "tools" whenever possible to describe what I'm offering; perhaps now, after you've made it nearly to the end, I should acknowledge what is probably already obvious to you: The tools provided are of two distinct types. First, I've described and discussed specific motivational "tools"—"schemes" might be a better term—such as pay for performance and goal-setting. But I've also offered conceptual tools or frameworks, ways of thinking about your relationship with your employees and their relationship with you, with your organization, and with their work. If applied with insight, these "thinking tools" will help you to understand the advantages and disadvantages of specific motivational strategies in your specific context. Kurt Lewin, one of the pioneers of social psychology and its application to management, famously said "Nothing is as practical as a good theory." As a management educator, I subscribe to this, although I would add to his aphorism: "Nothing is as practical as a good theory *intelligently applied*." I hope that the theories and frameworks I've provided are good. But it is up to you to apply them intelligently to your specific context.

This doesn't mean that there isn't generally applicable advice that I might give. I believe that organizations, and the people who run them, tend to have certain categories of "blinders" on when it comes to motivation. I've mentioned some of those in passing in previous chapters and, at the end of this chapter, I'll summarize the four items of significant general advice that, I believe, apply to many and perhaps most organizations.

But, before doing that, I would like to offer a different sort of assistance. Suppose you hired me as a consultant, with the general task of suggesting how to improve the motivation of your employees. The first thing I would do is ask you to answer a series of questions about your organization and its overall situation and environment. So, in this chapter, I'll go down a list of questions I would ask, together with explanations for why I think answers to those questions are key and how I might use some answers to provide you with advice. This is not a complete list of the questions I would ask you. Often, the answers you might give would inspire follow-on questions. But if you have absorbed the frameworks and ideas of this book, I believe that these questions, honestly answered by you after serious contemplation, will point you in the right direction.[1]

QUESTION SET I. What is your business strategy, and what role do your employees play in achieving that strategy? Are you eliciting the behavior you want? If so, how? If not, why not?

You might think answers to this question are so obvious that no retrospection is required. But, in my experience, being thoughtful and explicit about the link between strategy and employee efforts provides a lot of insight. Recall the story from Chapter 2 about the chain of health-food lunch shops, where managers at two different stores, given the incentive to raise the bottom-line results of their store, went in completely different directions. In the discussion back in Chapter 2, we took it as given that this was a bad outcome for the organization as a whole. But was it? This depends on the strategy of the organization as a whole: Is the chain's overall brand image important to it? Or would it be perfectly fine for the store in one location to have an entirely different look and feel from another location? Consistent brand image across locations is certainly important when a large proportion of the clientele at any one location are "drop-ins," brought into the restaurant location by some consistent brand image. But suppose instead that most customers in a location are customers only in that location and, moreover, are "regulars," who come to know the restaurant in their location from their experience in that location. Then the chain might well prefer that employees (in particular, managers at each location) undertake efforts to tailor what they do to the locals; if, say, one location serves primarily business people from a local office park, while another serves students from a nearby university, it may make sense to encourage distinct identities.*

Begin by identifying your organization's strategy. You can use whatever framework works for you, but if you want the framework that is taught to MBA students at Stanford GSB,[2] it involves answers to the following four questions:

1. What is the goal of the organization?

2. What is the scope of the organization's activities? What distinguishes it from its rivals, if anything? What is it *not* doing?

3. What is the source of its competitive advantage? What can it do that its rivals *cannot* (or cannot do *as well*), and why?

4. What is the logic that ties all this together? *Why* will the organization succeed in achieving its goals?

And, since we're concerned with employee motivation, add to these a fifth and sixth question:

---

* Although it is a bit off the point, I should add a follow-up question for this specific case: If the business strategy doesn't require consistency across different locations, what in the business strategy links different locations? To give a "for instance," it could be centralized procurement of raw materials. Whatever the answer, it is important to get it out on the table, because it may still have implications for what behavior is desired from employees.

5. What behaviors and actions by various employees are desired, to support and enhance your business strategy?

6. How do your HRM policies and practices elicit from your employees the desired behaviors and actions? How well do they do this?

For Question 5, different answers will of course be given for different groups or types of employees. Or, to put it the other way around, if you are concerned with the motivation of a specific group of employees, you should be answering Question 5 for that group. But beware the lesson from Artisans' Alliance: Even if your concern is with one type of employee, the answers to Question 6 for that type can be powerfully influenced by what you are doing in the realm of HRM with other types. (See Question Set III for more on this point.)

Also, for most organizations, the answers to Questions 1 through 4 drive the answers to Questions 5 and 6. You have a business strategy, and you motivate your employees to support that strategy. That is, the strategy comes first. This can be a trap. Depending on your situation and, in particular, the answers you give to some of the questions that follow, you might want to consider revising or even tailoring your business strategy, based on whom you employ, what is the employment environment, how your employees are attached to their work, and so forth.

That raises an important methodological point about this list of questions. I had to put them in some order, but don't be misled by that into thinking that once you've answered a question, you are done with it. As you answer a question further down on the list, you should ask yourself, *Does this suggest different answers to previous questions?* If I were helping you to think through your situation, I'd probably hear your answer to some question and say, "Given that, let's revisit what you said about . . ." You should do this on your own.

QUESTION SET II. What (if anything) is special about the economic, social, and legal environment within which you operate?

The *economic environment* in this question is not the market in which your products or services compete—those things enter into your business strategy—but instead the marketplace for labor services that you face and, then, the economic environment that faces your (prospective) employees. Contrast, for instance, the situation facing SAS Institute,[3] an enterprise-software firm located in Cary, North Carolina, with that facing one of its competitors located in Sunnyvale, California, in Silicon Valley. It is hardly true that Cary is located out in the "sticks"; it lies inside the Research Triangle formed by Durham, Chapel Hill, and Raleigh. But job-hopping—lateral movements by employees from one firm to another—is much less prevalent (and possible) in North Carolina than in Silicon Valley. Hence, SAS can and does use longer-term motivators with its employees. It invests heavily in its employees—providing "general-skills" training—investments that pay a return for SAS, with its very high retention rates, that is higher than would be the case for a firm in Silicon Valley, which might even lose an employee after providing general-skills training *because* that training makes the employee more desirable for other local firms. And you should also consider the condition of other markets in which your employees deal: The housing markets in and around Cary are very different from those in and around Sunnyvale; this can make quite a difference in how firms in the two locations structure benefits for incumbent employees and moving allowances for prospective employees from outside the region.

As for the social environment, consider for instance HRM practices that celebrate and recognize a single "Employee of the Month," meant both to motivate workers and to provide them with a concrete model of what sort of behavior is desired by the organization. In a culture that celebrates individual achievement—say, in Boston—this would fit a lot better than it would in Southeast Asia, where individuals strive not to stand out from their peers. (I have heard an anecdote, perhaps apocryphal, that when implementing an "Employee of the Month" program in rural Thailand, a company found that the unlucky winner was shunned and abused by his or her peers. The program was quickly discontinued.) Or, think of the differences in the social cultures of North Carolina and Silicon Valley and how those differences manifest themselves in the behavior of employees at SAS Institute versus, say, employees at Google.*

I doubt that I need to emphasize that HRM policies and practices in general need to fit with or, at least, take heed of the local market conditions and social environment. But general managers rarely appreciate the complexity of labor laws, at least in developed

---

* But—always a but—it should be noted that as Google started out, top management visited SAS Institute to see what they could learn from how SAS conducted its HRM. Google didn't copy SAS's policies and practices precisely, but adapted the good things that they saw at SAS to the different social and economic environment of Silicon Valley.

economies. Labor law in the United States is vast; moreover, it varies by state, with municipalities and cities sometimes adding more statutes related to worker rights. Of course, the elephant in the room—although it is found in increasingly fewer rooms—is organized labor; in the United States, organized labor (outside of certain geographic and industrial settings, and outside of the public sector) is unlikely to be a factor for you, but if your organization has a presence outside the United States, it can be significant. But, beyond organized labor, laws and regulations on what and how you pay employees, which benefits can be offered on a tax-preferred basis, and—with the advent of the Affordable Care Act and, as I write these lines, with whatever comes next—the rules around health care are many and complex.

Here are two specific examples that touch more or less directly on motivation:

- Using option grants or employee stock ownership schemes are clearly entangled by applicable law.

- Treating different groups of employees differently, either to defuse invidious social comparisons or simply because you want to motivate the groups differently, can run into laws against discrimination, especially with the rise of the disparate-impact doctrine.*

---

* The doctrine of disparate impact says that if actions you take affect different groups of employees differently, based simply on statistics, and, in particular, if "protected classes" of employees are adversely affected, those actions are discriminatory, even if you had no discriminatory intent. So, for instance, if you provide one group of employees with greater incentive compensation than a second group, because motivating members of the first group is more important to your bottom line, if the first group's average compensation is

Please note that I've phrased this question as, "*What (if anything) is special . . . ?*" I imagine that, for a lot of employers, the first reaction to this question is, "Nothing much is special." But, don't be fooled; instead dig deeper. There is probably more there that impinges on you than you initially realize.

QUESTION SET III. What is your work technology, broadly defined?

By the technology of work, I mean a lot more than: Is this a job-shop or an assembly-line process?; or How capital intensive is the process? When you think about "technology," think broadly, including answers to the following questions:

- What is the physical layout, including worker privacy and proximity to one another?

- What skills are required and how they are acquired?

- Concerning monitoring and measures of performance: Can employees be monitored directly? If so, how intrusive is it? What indirect measures of performance are

---

higher than the average for the second group in consequence, and the first group is disproportionately populated with men and the second group with women, you may be guilty of discrimination based on this doctrine. Or if you provide greater incentive payments for tasks that require greater upper-body strength, which will (probably) create adverse outcomes for women, you may be guilty based on this doctrine. As I write this, your defense in court is to show "business necessity" of the practices that led to the disparate impact; in both stories I've told, if your incentive schemes are economically sound, you might be okay. However, legal standards of what constitutes "business necessity" change with time and, I think it fair to say, have tended to become harder to meet.

available, to what extent do they reflect what the employees do? Are they observed with little or with long delay?

- How much creativity and proaction is required or desired, and how ambiguous (a priori) are the tasks to be done?

- To what extent does a single employee have responsibility for several tasks, who determines how the employee allocates his time among his tasks, and how do the different tasks vary in terms of all the dimensions listed here? (This is so important for motivation that it gets re-asked with greater emphasis later.)

- How interdependent are employee efforts?

- Touching both on interdependence and physical layout, which groups of employees interact on a day-to-day basis, and how do those interactions promote social comparisons (for good or for ill)? (Once again, the story of Artisans' Alliance illustrates why this question can be important.)

One dimension of technology that is particularly important when it comes to motivation and to HRM more generally concerns the relationship between performance of an individual employee and its impact on overall outcomes for the organization. (We covered this briefly in Chapter 6, but it is useful enough to present in detail here.) This mixes several of the dimensions of technology just mentioned, but often is a good way to summa-rize things:[4]

- A *star* job is one where mediocre or even poor perfor-mance by the employee doesn't have a significant neg-ative impact on the organization, but strong or even exceptional performance has an enormous positive impact. Think, for instance, of a researcher in a phar-maceutical company. If a bench scientist discovers a new and effective drug, it can be hugely profitable to the company; if a bench scientist tries a lot of things and comes up with nothing, it is costly, but not that costly in the grand scheme of things.

- At the other end of the spectrum, a *guardian* job is one where good performance moderately enhances the orga-nization's overall performance, while bad performance is a disaster for the organization. Think of a long-haul truck driver: It is good for the trucking firm if a driver does his job well, is efficient in getting from place to place on schedule (to the extent that he can control this), and so forth. But if he gets into a major accident—if, say, he is transporting chemicals and the accident causes those chemicals to spill into someone's drinking water supply—this can hugely harm the firm. (You might wonder about the bench scientist at a pharmaceuticals company who discovers a drug that turns out later to have devastating side-effects: Won't this dramatically and negatively hurt the company? It will, but while an individual bench scientist might play a key role in discovering a new drug, testing and certification is entirely a group effort.)

- Jobs in which good performance by the individual helps the organization, and bad performance hurts, but neither impact is dramatic, are called *foot soldier* jobs.

Please note that, in this classification system, it is the *job* and not the employee that is star, or guardian, or foot soldier. "She is a star employee" is a perfectly good English sentence, presumably meaning that she does her job in exemplary fashion. If she is driving a chemical carrier for the organization and does so with a spotless driving record while having the best on-time record of any driver in the company, she is a star truck driver. But her job, in this classification system, is still a *guardian job.*

And this matters because in terms of good HRM practice, what you do to recruit, train, monitor, evaluate, and motivate someone in a star job varies from how you do these things for a guardian job. For instance, in recruiting someone for a guardian job, you probably want to be very careful in terms of the individual's past work performance and references. You probably want to train the individual extensively. You want to motivate the person not to fail: The truck driver might be given some incentive to be on time, but it should be mild incentive and should allow for explanations of why the driver was late. For a star job, each of these is turned on its head: I wouldn't go so far as to say you want to seek out employees who will "gamble" in their efforts and then provide them with the motivation to do so, risking the strong likelihood of a bad outcome for a small chance of a very good one. But that isn't far off.

And, in some (usually the most problematic) cases, job designs are mixed *star-guardian* jobs, where exceptional performance on either end of the scale has huge consequences for the organization. Service jobs that call for creativity and proaction, but where the organization's reputation with its customer base is also important, often have this bad mix: Exceptional service can earn a lot of profit for the firm, but the employee who spends a disproportionate amount of time looking for the "home run" and so strikes out (screws up) the service of even a few customers can be a disaster.

QUESTION SET IV. What are your job designs?

Employees are put in jobs that are mixes of tasks. What are those mixes, and why have you created jobs with those mixes? As just said, jobs that mix star and guardian tasks are problematic. Back in Chapter 2, we discussed why motivation can be difficult for employees whose jobs mix tasks with quick-and-easy-to-measure performance and tasks for which it is difficult to measure performance, at least in a timely manner. There may be good reasons to bundle together tasks that mix these qualities into a single employee's job because the tasks are complementary, perhaps because of the employee's possession of relevant information, perhaps due to production technology. But you should not take job designs as given, and you should certainly be clear on the full list of tasks given to an employee before you set out to design his or her motivation. And if you do have job designs that mix hard-to-assess-performance tasks with easy-to-assess-performance tasks, this should certainly incline you toward the more psychology-based motivational tools.

QUESTION SET V. Who are your employees?

This set begins with classic demographic characteristics: *What is the age distribution of your employees? What are their educational backgrounds? How many are married and with children? How diverse are they, along multiple dimensions, including race, creed, gender, and ethnicity?* Few HRM policies and practices are universal in the sense that they work well for *every* workforce, and you want your practices to be well suited to the people who work for you. So, obviously, you want to know who they are.

Having said this, I must immediately issue a warning: Discrimination based on these demographic categories, either in hiring or in employment practices, can land you in legal hot water. When it comes to job interviews or even information gathering about current employees, certain questions cannot be asked. There are cases where demographic discrimination in hiring is permitted; when membership in a demographic group can be shown (in court) to be a bona fide occupational qualification. But those cases are hard to make; an understanding of the law, which may require consultation with a good labor lawyer, is essential.

And, beyond your legal obligations: While "you want your HRM practices to be well suited to the people who work for you" is good advice, it can be dangerous advice if you, like most people, are subject to prejudices about the tastes and behaviors of different demographic groups. Such prejudices can seem scientific, based on statistics properly applied to samples of past workers who are relatively homogeneous.* But often they are based on the blind application of faulty folk wisdom.

Consider, for instance, Sun Hydraulics, a firm that manufactures and designs fluid-power devices (hydraulic valves and manifolds), headquartered in Sarasota, Florida.† Sun was founded by Robert Koski, who held contrarian views about the behavior and motivation of skilled blue-collar workers, among other management matters. The production technology for producing hydraulic valves and manifolds is pure job-shop: Highly skilled blue-collar workers use general-purpose machine tools to convert raw materials into finished products, involving for each product a complex sequence of steps that varies from product to product. Folk wisdom is that job-shop operations live or die by (a) scheduling work skillfully, which is, per folk wisdom, beyond the capabilities of the blue-collar fabricators, and (b) closely supervising the blue-collar fabricators, again based on folk wisdom about the behavior of this class of employees. Koski believed that this was

---

* The problem here is one of sample size. If the data you process about, say, voluntary quits by men and women is based on historical records where you've employed many more men than women, and you are looking to fill a job where you want to be relatively sure that the person will not leave, the small sample size of women will mean less assurance in your estimate. For more on this, see Baron and Kreps, *Strategic Human Resources: Frameworks for General Managers* (New York: Wiley, 1999), p. 353ff.

† Sun Hydraulics, a fascinating company, is the subject of a superb series of Harvard Business School cases. If I can convince you to study the details of one company, to expand your ideas about employee motivation (and employee behavior, more generally), it is to study Sun. To get started, consult Louis B. Barnes and Colleen Kaftan, "Sun Hydraulics Corporation (A and B) (Abridged)," Harvard Business School Case 9-491-119. But don't stop there—in particular, see follow-up cases about how Sun dealt with the recessions of 2001 and 2008.

hokum, that his blue-collar workers, treated with the respect they deserved both for their skills and for their knowledge, could do a much better job if provided with all the information they needed to self-schedule and self-supervise. ("Self" here may be a bit of a misnomer: Peer pressure among the blue-collar workers at Sun is probably ferocious. The point is that white-collar scheduling and supervision is at least unnecessary and perhaps suboptimal.) The history of Sun certainly indicates that Koski was right and folk wisdom about the nature of high-skill blue-collar workers was, at least in this case, wrong. And lest you think this is something only true about highly skilled blue-collar workers, ServiceMaster is a successful company founded on HRM principles very similar to those of Sun, but for semi- and unskilled blue-collar workers.*

Compiling demographic statistics about your workforce is important, but it is just the beginning of answering the question, *Who are your employees?* Go back to Chapter 5. Are your employees' connections to their work and their jobs instrumental or expressive? If they are expressive, what is the nature of the expressive connection? Are your employees work driven? Values driven? Mission driven? Driven by the success of the organization? Cutting this along a somewhat different dimension, do your employees regard their relationship with your organization as a job, a career, or a calling?

One way to understand what Koski achieved at Sun Hydraulics employs these categories. The folk wisdom about the behavior of blue-collar workers may be accurate to the extent that blue-

---

* Look on the Web for the page that describes ServiceMaster's organizational culture, http://www.servicemaster.com/about-us/we-serve.

collar workers have a largely instrumental connection to their work and to the organization for which they work. The blue-collar workers at Sun, however, have a much stronger and expressive connection to the work they do and to the organization for which they work, which changes how they behave on the job; Koski's insight was to understand that building this sort of connection was possible by treating this group of employees with respect and by giving them autonomy over their day-to-day activities.

I doubt that any set of questions, except perhaps for the question linking business strategy to desired employee behavior, are more deserving of deep reflection than questions about how employees connect psychologically to what they do on the job. The response of your employees to different motivational tools you can employ will be profoundly affected by the answers. The sad story of Artisans' Alliance is another good case in point; for still another, consider furniture maker Herman Miller.[5] Herman Miller (HM) is best known for its office furniture, including such iconic pieces as the Eames chair, the Aeron chair, and the Action Office modular office system. Manufacturing takes place in Zeeland, Michigan, with a workforce that is strongly evangelical Christian in the Reformed Protestant tradition. The firm celebrates these values, honoring employees for and giving them paid time off to engage in community service. Employees at HM are at least values driven, and a case can be made that they are mission driven, where the company's mission statement is "Inspiring designs to help people do great things." All this has resulted in employees who are able—and willing, and expected—to take part in the day-to-day management of factory-floor operations.

For a variety of reasons, HM decided in 2012 to undertake a major strategic initiative. This included expanding the scope of operations, both in terms of product and, importantly, geography. Expansion was achieved through acquisition, and geographic expansion involved acquiring a Chinese office-furniture manufacturing company, POSH Office Systems. POSH is described as a "very traditional Chinese company," which means, with employees whose relationship to their company is very different from the relationship of HM and its core employees. As you would expect, the acquisition of a company with such a different employee-employer relationship raises issues of whether HM should try to keep POSH as it is or remodel it along HM lines and, if it decides to change POSH, how and how fast. Making these decisions, in turn, requires that HM understand how POSH employees are attached to their jobs, their work, and their employer.

But it is not HM's relationship with its new employees at POSH that motivates the telling of this story. Instead, consider how HM's actions at POSH might affect its relationship with its core workforce back in Michigan. Those workers share values and even a mission with HM. Suppose they misinterpret what HM is doing in China. Suppose HM does not try to change the employee-employer relationship at POSH, and the employees back in Zeeland recognize this and decide that this is not in accord with the values they thought they shared with HM. Or suppose that the employees in Zeeland are simply kept guessing about HM's intentions in China. In any of these circumstances, the psychological contract between HM and its core workforce— which is worth a great deal to HM in terms of management and motivation—could be badly damaged.* This is an ongoing story, so we don't know how it will end. But it should be clear that top management at HM, in deciding what to do in China, must consider the impact on employee attitudes back home. And they must go out of their way to keep their core workforce informed and "on the same page" concerning the strategic initiative and the details of its implementation.

This story suggests the next set of questions you should ask yourself:

QUESTION SET VI. Are you and your employees on the same page?

If your employees were asked the questions in Question Sets I through III, would their answers be consistent with the answers you gave? In other words, are you and they on the same page concerning: (1) your business strategy; (2) their role in that strategy; (3) their relationship with you, your organization, and their jobs; and (4) the details, explicit but especially implicit, of how employment "works" at your organization? And, how do they feel about these things? In particular, do they believe that your policies and practices are equitable and, where they do not believe this, what is the source of their dissatisfaction?

If your employment relationship is, for your employees, a one-

---

* Sales per employee in 2011 at HM were around $250,000, while sales per employee at POSH were around $40,000. Of course, this doesn't tell the whole story: Presumably, the levels of capital intensity are very different, these are measures of average and not marginal productivity, and employee salaries are bound to be different. But the scale of the difference is striking, indicating that HM should be very concerned with its relationship with its core workforce.

off, instrumental transaction—they work, they get paid—then you can probably make do with relative ignorance on their part, as long as they understand what they are meant to do and how they will be compensated. But if you have the sort of long-term relationship described in Chapter 4, and especially if you have a psychological "contract" with your employees in the sense of Chapters 5 and 6, you are courting trouble if their understanding doesn't match yours. And, in many cases, employers are surprised by how poor is their employees' understanding of what the employer was sure is common knowledge.

Obviously, you want to communicate these things to them. But you should also listen to them, in direct conversation and via anonymous feedback platforms.

One more question connected to *Who are your employees?* should be addressed:

QUESTION SET VII. What about your pool of job applicants?

Are your HRM policies and practices attractive to the "right sort" of *prospective* employees? Are they attractive to the "wrong sort?" (In both cases, how and why?) To what extent are your HRM policies and practices appreciated by prospective employees? To what extent do your recruiting practices present an honest and complete picture of what employment with your organization means?

These questions may be difficult to answer, because you don't have ready access to prospective employees who do not become employees. You can interview your (newly arrived) employees and ask them, "What did you know about us when you were thinking of coming to work here?" But, of course, the fact that they chose to work for you makes them a biased sample. You'd like to ask those who chose to work somewhere else, "Why?" And, hardest of all, you'd like to ask those who chose not to apply at all, "Why not?" But how do you do this? You could ask a consumer-marketing survey firm (or your own consumer-marketing survey people, if you employ such specialists) to run a survey that asks, "Have you ever considered working at [insert name of your organization]? If not, why not? And what do you know about working conditions there?" But will the data be worth the cost?

One indication that you need help on this front is the percentage of new hires who quickly become ex-hires. Exit interviews with voluntary quits, and, in particular, short-term voluntary quits, can be very enlightening.

QUESTION SET VIII. How well do your different HRM policies and practices fit together?

When it comes to HRM, individual policies and practices, including those directed at motivation, perform better or worse—defined in terms of how well they support the organization's strategy—to the extent that they fit together.

Partly, this is technological: For instance, if the organization gives employees a lot of on-the-job autonomy with little oversight, even though it could monitor and direct them closely, it will do better to the extent that employees are recruited with care and are given appropriate training. Careful recruitment and training can be costly, so this goes together with HRM practices that reduce voluntary turnover. Or, to take another example, if a particular job is purely a star job, one wants (a) to motivate in a way that encourages employees to take risks and, simultaneously, (b) to hire broadly on the basis of potential. For jobs where teamwork is crucial, rewarding individual performance can be counterproductive, and hiring for cultural fit becomes very important. Perhaps the most commonly observed technological connection concerns training and turnover: An organization that devotes a lot of resources to training its employees will typically wish to embrace policies that reduce voluntary turnover, so it can get a good return on its training investment.

A second benefit of consistency concerns the psychology of perception and cognition. Of course, organizations have formal rules, processes, and procedures. But especially for the open-ended employment relationships of Chapter 4, organizations rely on relational contracts with employees; employees should know what is expected of them in various circumstances and should proceed on that basis. And they should have a clear and accurate view of what they can expect, in return. If different HRM practices send mixed messages about what the organization expects and how it reciprocates, it is harder for employees to get this right in specific cases. To the extent that HRM practices are consistent in philosophy or spirit or underlying principles, employees are more likely to get it right in any specific instance. For supervisory employees—think of Bob's immediate boss Alice—this can be very important: Alice makes day-to-day decisions that affect Bob and that Bob perceives to some extent as decisions made by Zephyr Corporation. Zephyr wants Alice to have a very clear idea of what she should do in specific situations ("should" here meaning "consistent with Zephyr's overall reputation with Bob and his peers") and the more that Zephyr's HRM practices that Alice must implement are thematically consistent, the more likely it is that she'll make the right decisions.

This reason extends to fit with the larger social and cultural environment. If all of what goes on inside the organization in terms of HRM is consistent with some general external social relationship—which could be a family, or an "all-is-fair" marketplace, or (for engineers) the university department at which they were students or even faculty members—employees will come to understand the organization and the part they play within it more accurately and quickly. And, of course, pieces of HRM practice that are individually consistent with some external social structure are likely to be consistent with one another.

To the extent that an organization has HRM practices that fit in this sense—that are consistent both internally and with other aspects of the organization—the recruitment of new employees can be aided, especially insofar as prospective employees can learn about the organization before they apply for a job. SAS Institute in North Carolina and Sun Hydraulics in Florida both have suites of HRM policies and practices that are very well known locally (and, in the case of Sun, to the international community of hydraulics engineers). Prospective employees can and do self-select—those who think they will fit look for jobs with these firms, while those who think they will not fit look elsewhere—which of course benefits the respective organizations.

The discussion so far has concerned consistency across different pieces of HRM, such as consistency of training policies with policies that discourage voluntary turnover, or between selection criteria and level of supervision and direction. Two other dimensions of consistency of HRM practice are worth mentioning:

1. You should think about *consistency of practices across different categories of employees.* Some organizations strive to treat all their employees on a largely consistent basis. Others make clear distinctions. Where there are clear social distinctions, this sort of inconsistency of practice is easier to sustain. When the social distinctions are not there, the company may want to invent them. For instance, when IBM built a group to design the early PCs, it decided that the white-shirt-only, strictly regimented culture and accompanying HRM practices that were hallmarks of IBM would be counterproductive to what IBM desired these employees to do. So it went out of its way to house the new group in a location where there would be little interaction with the bulk of the (then) mainframe-oriented workforce.

   Or, put negatively, think of Artisans' Alliance. It put in place a vastly different compensation system for its sales reps, without creating sufficient distinctions between the sales reps and the other professionals in the firm. Whether it would have been better for AA not to use such a different compensation system or to try to build "walls" between the two groups is open to debate. But, doing neither, it got a bad outcome.

2. Especially when it comes to the more implicit aspects of HRM policies and practices, *consistency over time* can be

very important. For one thing, consistency of behavior over time is crucial to any effective reputation; a reputation for acting one way on Monday, Wednesday, and Friday and a different way on Tuesday and Thursday is unlikely to be understood and, therefore, will be unsustainable. And, even if we are talking only of a once-and-for-all switch, when the switch is made, employees are likely to be unclear about what to expect, at least for a while.

Moreover, the problems arising from inconsistency over time in HRM policies and practices goes beyond employee confusion and expectations for the future. Recall the story of Beth Israel Hospital from Chapter 6: Over many years, Beth Israel built up a very effective implicit contract with its senior RNs. In exchange for giving the nurses an unusually large role in managing the care of "their" patients, it got truly extraordinary performance from them. Then, financial pressures on hospitals generally left this hospital with a choice of practices that would, at best, chip away at and, at worst, completely remove this large role from the RN's job. The reason that the nurses provided truly exceptional performance in the "old" environment was largely psychological; removing the RN's autonomy and ability to manage their patients' care therefore meant breaking a psychological contract, eliciting (predictably) a very strongly negative emotional reaction from the nurses.

Another problem arising from inconsistency over

time is captured by the term *punctuated equilibrium*, taken from the literature of evolutionary biology.* In terms of HRM, an organization and its employees may reach an equilibrium of understandings: The organization expects A, employees provide B, the organization reciprocates with C and D. If the organization suddenly announces that it will reciprocate with C and E (to give an example from the folklore of Silicon Valley, if the company was providing refrigerators stocked with any beverages chosen by employees and announces that, henceforth, only three specific beverages will be provided) the employees question the entire equilibrium. "Is C still going to be provided? Should we provide less than B? Perhaps, since E is less than D, the company is obligated to adjust downward *its* expectations of what we provide?" The point is, when a long-standing and well-understood equilibrium has been modified in one dimension, the entire equilibrium has been punctured, and participants think that every aspect of the equilibrium should be up for renegotiation. So be careful in changing one piece of practice. You may unwittingly be putting everything on the table.

---

* In biology, the adjective *punctuated* refers to the notion that, in a formerly stable ecology, changing one aspect can disrupt the ecological equilibrium, causing a rapid burst of evolutionary activity until a new equilibrium is reached. Hence, evolutionary activity is marked by long stretches of relative stability, punctuated with rapid bursts to accommodate any changes. In this setting, where the "equilibrium" can be changed by an act of management, the term *punctured* equilibrium might be more suitable.

QUESTION SET IX. How about your organization culture(s)?

Is there an overall organizational culture and, if so, what is it? If there are separate cultures among different groups of employees, what are they? How do your motivational schemes affect the culture(s), for good and for bad?

Organizational culture is a summary of how the members of your organization relate to their work, their jobs, the organization, each other, and to other constituencies of your organization, including suppliers and customers. In a sense, this question, together with the question about your business strategy, are bookends for all the other questions. The questions about business strategy concern what you and your organization are trying to achieve, and why you think you can achieve those things; those questions bias you toward thinking of your organization as an entity with a purpose. On the other end of the spectrum, you should think of your organization as a "marketplace" in which individuals—the focus here is on your employees—exchange economic and social goods. Your organizational culture aims at a succinct description of the way in which those individuals relate to these exchanges.

Often, an organization doesn't have a single culture in these terms; but instead different groups of employees have distinct cultures. For instance, based on my personal experience, tenure-track faculty members and adjunct faculty members at Stanford GSB have different cultures, and the many different types of support personnel—clerical support, the development and alumni support teams, the student-service teams—each have cultures with some distinct elements. That's not necessarily a bad thing; it is in fact a natural outcome given differences in who they are in terms of demography, education, and social background; what they do; the labor markets they face; and so forth. But in thinking about motivating your employees, it is important that you acknowledge these differences and, in particular, the role that your motivational schemes play in creating, supporting, and, sometimes, grinding against the culture or cultures within your organization.

After answering all the previous questions, you may find the answer to this question to be, "There is no succinct description of the organizational culture or the various subcultures within my organization." In my view, this answer should raise a red flag. At least when it comes to Type-K employees, I would read the "no easy answer" response as a signal that, in economic terms, your employment relationships are not constructed on a solid base of mutual understanding and, in social-psychological terms, your employees probably have tenuous connections to their jobs and the organization. While I'm not saying that "no easy answer" necessarily implies these dangers, it worries me, and I think it should worry you.

Final Words of Wisdom

These nine sets of questions, answered after serious contemplation, would help me as an outsider to understand your situation as it relates to the management of your human resources and, in particular, the challenges you face and opportunities you have for motivating your employees. If you take the time—and, when it

comes to ascertaining what your employees think, the resources—
to answer them for yourself, you will have clarified those challenges and, I hope, some opportunities. Because there are so many
different ways to motivate your workforce, I am reluctant to suggest any in particular to you; I hope that the frameworks I have
presented and anecdotes I have related in the course of describing
different motivational schemes will allow you to invent a scheme
that works well for you.

There are, however, some general tendencies in organizations
that are trying to motivate their employees, which I present below,
along with some general advice. You may not need this advice;
many well-run organizations and wise managers know these
things already. But based on my experiences interacting with
senior managers, mostly in executive education programs, here
are four insights that seem to produce a lot of "Aha!" moments:

1. Is "interesting work" the magic bullet?

Recall Tables 2 and 4 from Chapter 3, which give results of my
surveys of SEP participants and MBA students concerning five
motivational channels, both in terms of how the participants/
students rate each channel and then which channel is most
descriptive of their organization (in the case of SEP participants)
or last job (for the MBA students). For your convenience, they are
reproduced here.

The winner in almost every case is "interesting and exciting
work." For the SEP participants' own motivation, "contributing to
organization success" barely beats "interesting and exciting work"
for most descriptive, but in every other case, "interesting and

Table 2. Responses from SEP Participants on the Five Motivational Channels

(a) Which channel is most descriptive

	Tangible rewards; e.g., pay	Intangible personal rewards; e.g., praise	Interesting & exciting work	Contributes to organizational success	Contributes to greater social purpose
For self	15.5%	11.1%	25.6%	27.5%	20.3%
For direct reports	17.4%	20.2%	26.6%	23.7%	12.1%

(b) Self scores

	Tangible rewards; e.g., pay	Intangible personal rewards; e.g., praise	Interesting & exciting work	Contributes to organizational success	Contributes to greater social purpose
Not at all effective	0.5%	0.0%	0.0%	0.0%	1.0%
Limited effectiveness	6.3%	3.9%	0.5%	1.0%	10.6%
Effective, but not very	30.9%	17.9%	5.3%	6.8%	29.0%
Very effective	33.8%	41.5%	29.0%	32.4%	31.4%
Extremely effective	27.5%	32.4%	58.0%	52.7%	24.6%
Only this is effective	1.0%	4.3%	7.2%	7.2%	3.4%
Mean	3.85	4.15	4.66	4.58	3.78
Standard deviation	0.95	0.71	0.76	1.07	0.90

(c) Scores for direct reports

	Tangible rewards; e.g., pay	Intangible personal rewards; e.g., praise	Interesting & exciting work	Contributes to organizational success	Contributes to greater social purpose
Not at all effective	0.0%	0.0%	0.0%	0.0%	0.5%
Limited effectiveness	8.7%	1.0%	1.9%	2.9%	20.3%
Effective, but not very	29.0%	21.3%	4.8%	20.8%	40.1%
Very effective	40.1%	49.3%	37.7%	44.0%	25.6%
Extremely effective	21.3%	27.5%	51.2%	30.9%	13.0%
Only this is effective	1.0%	1.0%	4.3%	1.4%	0.5%
Mean	3.77	4.06	4.51	4.07	3.32
Standard deviation	0.91	0.75	0.74	0.83	0.97

Table 4. MBA-Student Responses to the Five-Motivational-Channel Questions

(a) Which channel is most descriptive

	Tangible rewards; e.g., pay	Intangible personal rewards; e.g., praise	Interesting & exciting work	Contributes to organizational success	Contributes to greater social purpose
For self	14.6%	28.8%	37.9%	7.9%	10.8%
For peers	28.8%	22.1%	34.2%	4.6%	10.4%

(b) Self scores

	Tangible rewards; e.g., pay	Intangible personal rewards; e.g., praise	Interesting & exciting work	Contributes to organizational success	Contributes to greater social purpose
Not at all effective	0.4%	0.0%	0.4%	2.1%	5.0%
Limited effectiveness	7.5%	2.9%	0.8%	15.4%	13.8%
Effective, but not very	25.0%	9.6%	6.3%	25.4%	26.7%
Very effective	39.6%	32.1%	18.3%	35.0%	28.3%
Extremely effective	26.3%	52.5%	65.8%	20.8%	22.9%
Only this is effective	1.3%	2.9%	8.3%	1.3%	3.3%
Mean	3.88	4.43	4.73	3.61	3.60
Standard deviation	0.94	0.81	0.76	1.08	1.21

(c) Scores for peers

	Tangible rewards; e.g., pay	Intangible personal rewards; e.g., praise	Interesting & exciting work	Contributes to organizational success	Contributes to greater social purpose
Not at all effective	0.4%	0.0%	0.0%	2.5%	5.0%
Limited effectiveness	4.6%	1.7%	1.3%	19.6%	26.3%
Effective, but not very	20.8%	12.5%	9.6%	36.3%	30.0%
Very effective	38.8%	45.0%	35.8%	27.1%	27.9%
Extremely effective	33.8%	40.4%	49.2%	14.6%	10.4%
Only this is effective	1.7%	0.4%	4.2%	0.0%	0.4%
Mean	4.06	4.25	4.45	3.32	3.14
Standard deviation	0.95	0.74	0.83	1.02	1.10

exciting work" is the leader, for both self-motivation and for peers or direct reports.

And not only that: Look at the percentages of respondents who say that "interesting and exciting work" is at least "very effective": for the SEP participants about themselves, 94.2%; for the SEP participants about their direct reports, 93.2%; for the MBA students about themselves, 92.4%; and for the MBA students about their peers, 89.2%. This shouldn't be surprising: Giving someone work that they find interesting and exciting is, by itself, powerfully motivating; it is the motivational magic bullet.

There are three obvious problems with this finding: First, sometimes work must be done that is neither interesting nor exciting. Second, employees who find a particular project interesting and exciting may take things too far, spending too much of their time on that project when there are other tasks to do.* Third, and

---

* Jim Baron, Diane Burton, and Michael Hannan conducted an empirical study of high-tech start-ups in Silicon Valley, in which (among other things) they looked at how the "HRM vision" of the organization correlated with firm performance. The dimensions of HRM vision that they used were only indirectly about motivation of the workforce but, reading a bit between the lines, what they called a "star organization" could reasonably be identified as an organization in which "do great technical work" was the chief motivator. And they found that, while these organizations did not do best in terms of economic and financial performance (versus other types of organizations), they did do best if one looked only at those start-ups that made it to the stage of initial public offering. I believe that we are looking here at a variant of the well-known adage: "the perfect is the enemy of good." When, in these organizations, motivation chiefly stemmed from doing a great (technical) job—when motivation was via interesting and exciting work—the engineers and scientists who were "inventing" the product would often ignore market realities to get to the most beautiful and scientifically excellent product. By looking at firms that made it to IPO, they filtered out of their sample the beautiful failures, at least to some extent. Moral: Interesting and exciting work is a great motivator. But not when it leads employees to ignore the economic reasons for the work being done.
  A good, nontechnical summary of this research can be found in Baron and Hannan, "Organizational Blueprints for Success in High-Tech Start-Ups: Lessons from the Stanford Project on Emerging Companies" (*California Management Review*, Vol. 44, 2002, 8–36). If you have any interest in HRM in start-ups and, in particular, in high-tech start-ups, you should read this wonderful article.

another way in which things can be taken too far, employees may keep working on an interesting and exciting project past the point where a good-enough job has been done. These problems all come down to your employee having *too much* motivation to do what he or she finds interesting and exciting, spending more time and effort on that task while avoiding or shirking other tasks.

These are real problems. But in my experience, with a Type-K employee, a good motivational practice is to sit down and try to identify tasks that (1) he or she would like to do, and (2) that will benefit the organization if done well. When you can find tasks that satisfy both these criteria—and they exist more often than you might think, if you and your employee look hard for them—the motivation to provide consummate effort will flow nearly effortlessly.

2. Are you trying too hard?

Motivation in this book has been formulated as "aligning the interests of the employee with his or her employer." "Aligning" in this formulation suggests that it is something you must actively do; that in the natural state of affairs, your employees' interests will not be aligned with your own, and you need to do something about that.

It isn't necessarily so. And if it is so, it may not be necessary for you to do much. Especially when it comes to Type-K employees, their intrinsic motivation is often to do good work and be seen doing good work, to contribute to the success of the team, and to be respected and even admired for what they do. These intrinsic motivations may be enough, and if you pile on motivation by other means, you can dull the naturally occurring intrinsic motivation.

Of course, your employees need to know what they should be doing to help the organization achieve its goals. It helps if you take steps so that the individual employee internalizes the success of the organization as his or her own success; to the extent possible, you should promote the notion of the employee as teammate or "owner."

But always consider that in the context of motivation, less is *sometimes* more.

3. Is your list of rewards too short?

If rewards are needed, think broadly in terms of what rewards you can provide. Go back to Table 5 and the notion that intrinsic rewards may work better on your employees than you (at first) think. Consider goal-setting and achievement of a SMART goal as a reward. Consider self-determination theory and psychological motivators in general. Sometimes, money—or the prospect of promotion—is the most effective tool. This is particularly true in organizational and social cultures where the rule is that "he who dies with the most toys, wins." But that is not a universal rule; it is probably less of a rule than most managers believe.

4. Are you too concerned with today's problem?

One suggestion that I've made several times in this book is to always think about the longer-term and broader-scope implications of how you are motivating your employees. Too often, the demands of the here and now or this specific case overwhelm longer-term and broader-scope considerations, to the detriment of the organization. Assuming you have a long-term relationship with the employee with whom you are dealing today, and assuming that what you do with or about or for this employee will have repercussions for your relationship with your other employees, you need to be as mindful of the future as you are of the present.

And finally:

I return to Chapter 1 and the wisdom of Robert Bass. Management is, in most contexts, first and foremost about getting things done through the efforts of others. Rather than trying to control your employees through specific dos and don'ts, your job is to find people who can excel and unleash their passion and creativity in productive directions. Align their interests with yours—motivate them—and you will reap the rewards together.

APPENDIX.
THE WISDOM OF CROWDS:
WHAT DO MANAGERS BELIEVE?

I n this appendix, I present in greater depth the results of the surveys of Stanford Executive Program (SEP) participants and Stanford GSB MBA students concerning what they think about different motivators. To keep the narrative flow, I will in places repeat things already described in the previous chapters. The discussion is lengthy and, in places, may tend to be soporific; in case you find yourself falling asleep, a short executive summary is included at the end.

The surveys are described in bits and pieces in the text, but to summarize: Two slightly different surveys were administered to two groups: participants in the Stanford Executive Program (SEP), a six-week, open-enrollment executive program; and MBA students who were enrolled in a first-year course I taught in Human Resource Management (HRM). In each case, the data I will present are from two years, the SEP of summers 2014 and 2015, and the MBA student classes of 2015 and 2016. The survey of the SEP participants was administered on their first three days of the program, before any of the issues with which the survey is concerned were discussed in the program; the survey of MBA students was administered over the break between winter and spring quarters, before the start of the HRM course. The MBA students (for the most part) had just completed a course in microeconomics in which the economic theory of incentives—the stuff of Chapter 2—had been discussed, and the students knew that I am an economist by affiliation, so while the surveys were administered anonymously, the students were probably biased towards economics-style incentives, if they were biased at all. The response rate among the SEP participants was around 60% (n = 207), and the response rate among the MBAs was around 80% (n = 240), although you should bear in mind that the survey was offered only to MBA students who chose to take a course in HRM, which may not be a representative sample of all Stanford GSB MBA students.

Demographic characteristics of the responding populations are given in Table 1 and Table 3; to summarize, the SEP participants were global senior executives (30% United States/Canada; 28% Europe; 22% South Asia/East Asia), with a median age of approximately 45, a median rank of senior VP/partner, mostly general managers, largely (86%) male, with substantial representation in financial services (17.9%), IT/electronics/computers (23.2%), and manufacturing/construction (14.5%). The MBA students were largely from United States/Canada (71%), fairly well balanced between men and women, median age in the late 20s (80% between 26 and 30), with largest representation in terms of functional specialty in general management (25%), finance (24%), and strategy (20%), and with the largest representation in terms of industry of their last job in the financial services sector (24%) and consulting (20%).

The Survey Instrument

On the following pages, the survey given to the SEP participants is reproduced. (There were slight differences in the survey given to MBA students, which will be noted.) The survey had three parts. Part I asked the participants to provide demographic information: Geographical location of their home base, age, sex, rank, functional specialty, and sector or industry of their organization. For the MBAs, organizational rank was replaced by undergraduate major, and they were told that all questions about their "organization" meant the organization at which they last worked before starting the MBA program. Percentage responses for the two groups are recorded in Tables 1 and 3, on pages 60 and 64 of the text.

Part II of the surveys concerned the five motivational channels discussed in Chapter 3. This part began with the following preamble:

> The next four questions concern what motivates "best work" or "consummate effort" in your organization back home. To be clear, by best work or consummate effort, I mean effort that goes above and beyond the nominal specs of the job. I'm interested both in what motivates you and in what motivates your direct reports, and in this part of the survey, I am interested in the following five sorts of motivators:
>
> a. A direct connection between providing consummate effort and tangible rewards for the individual, such as a bigger bonus, higher pay, and better promotion prospects.

b. A direct connection between proving consummate effort and intangible rewards for the individual that, while intangible, come from others, such as praise or enhanced status and respect among co-workers.

c. Work that is personally interesting and exciting.

d. A direct connection between providing consummate effort and success for the organization (or work group).

e. Work that contributes to society, transcending both the personal interests and rewards of the individual doing the work and the well-being of associates and the organization for which the individual works.

Then came the questions:

7. *Think about the people who report directly to you. How effective (generally) are each of the five sorts of motivators, in eliciting from them their very best (consummate) work?*

	Not effective at all	Of limited effectiveness	Effective, but not very effective	Very effective	Extremely effective	This, and this alone, is effective in eliciting very best (consummate) work
A direct connection between providing consummate effort and tangible rewards for them.	O	O	O	O	O	O
A direct connection between providing consummate effort and intangible rewards from others, such as praise.	O	O	O	O	O	O
Work that is personally interesting/exciting.	O	O	O	O	O	O
A direct connection between providing consummate effort and success for the organization.	O	O	O	O	O	O
Work that contributes to the broader society.	O	O	O	O	O	O

8. *For the people who report directly to you, which of the following statements is MOST descriptive of what motivates their best work?*

○ My direct reports do their best work when they can see a clear connection with tangible rewards for themselves, such as a bigger bonus, higher pay, etc.

○ My direct reports do their best work when they can see a clear connection with intangible rewards, such as praise and/or enhanced status and respect among co-workers.

○ My direct reports do their best work when they find the work interesting and exciting to them personally.

○ My direct reports do their best work when they understand that the work is important to the success of the organization (or work group).

○ My direct reports do their best work because they consider their work to be an important mission that transcends their own personal interests and rewards and the well-being of their associates and the organization for which they work.

9. *Of course, people differ in what motivates them, and your answers to Questions 7 and 8 may not do justice to the variety of motivations of your direct reports. In this respect, which of the following statements best describes your situation?*

○ My direct reports tend to be quite different in what motivates their best work. I find that I must vary the techniques used to motivate my direct reports to get the best results.

○ While my direct reports differ in what motivates their best work, I find that I can (and do) tend to motivate them in largely similar ways.

○ My direct reports are very similar in what motivates their best work, so I can treat them the same when it comes to motivating them.

Part II continued with questions about the respondents themselves:

10. *Now think about yourself. How effective (generally) are each of the five sets of motivators, in eliciting your own very best (consummate) work?*

	Not effective at all	Of limited effectiveness	Effective, but not very effective	Very effective	Extremely effective	This, and this alone is effective in eliciting very best (consummate) work
A direct connection between providing consummate effort and tangible rewards for me.	○	○	○	○	○	○
A direct connection between providing consummate effort and intangible rewards from others, such as praise or enhanced status/respect among co-workers.	○	○	○	○	○	○
Work that is personally interesting/exciting.	○	○	○	○	○	○
A direct connection between providing consummate effort and success for the organization.	○	○	○	○	○	○
Work that contributes to the broader society.	○	○	○	○	○	○

11. *Finally, which of the following is MOST descriptive of what motivates your own best work?*

○ I do my best work when there is a clear connection between superior performance and tangible rewards for me, such as higher pay, a larger bonus, better promotion prospects, and so forth.

○ I do my best work when I can see a clear connection with intangible rewards from others, such as praise and/or enhanced status and respect among co-workers.

○ I do my best work when the work involved is interesting and exciting to me personally.

○ I do my best work when I understand that superior performance is important to the success of the organization (or work group).

○ I do my best work because I consider my work to be an important mission that transcends my own personal interests and rewards and the well-being of their associates and the organization for which I work.

And then came Part III, concerning the eight types of motivator discussed in Chapter 5.[1] This began with a preamble:

The final part of the survey concerns eight general categories of motivator, slicing things differently from in Part II. The eight categories we consider in this part are:

1. Benefits (such as health care, retirement benefits, etc.)

2. Feeling good about the work you do, how you do it, etc.

3. The ability to learn and grow on the job

4. Pay, in all its various forms, including salaries, bonus, etc.

5. Praise received for a job well done, whether from board members, fellow workers, subordinates, the press, etc.

6. Job security

7. The opportunity to acquire and practice skills

8. The opportunity to do truly worthwhile things

12. *How much of an impact does each category of motivator have on you, personally, in your job? Please answer on the seven-point scale shown.*

	No impact on me or my behavior	Negligible impact	Limited impact	Moderate impact	Substantial impact	Powerful impact	I live and die according to this motivator
Benefits	◯	◯	◯	◯	◯	◯	◯
Feeling good	◯	◯	◯	◯	◯	◯	◯
Learn and grow	◯	◯	◯	◯	◯	◯	◯
Pay	◯	◯	◯	◯	◯	◯	◯
Praise	◯	◯	◯	◯	◯	◯	◯
Job security	◯	◯	◯	◯	◯	◯	◯
Acquire and practice skills	◯	◯	◯	◯	◯	◯	◯
Do worthwhile things	◯	◯	◯	◯	◯	◯	◯

13. *How strong is the impact of each category of motivator on your peers and/or direct reports "back home"?*

	No impact on them or their behavior	Negligible impact	Limited impact	Moderate impact	Substantial impact	Powerful impact	They live and die according to this motivator
Benefits	◯	◯	◯	◯	◯	◯	◯
Feeling good	◯	◯	◯	◯	◯	◯	◯
Learn and grow	◯	◯	◯	◯	◯	◯	◯
Pay	◯	◯	◯	◯	◯	◯	◯
Praise	◯	◯	◯	◯	◯	◯	◯
Job security	◯	◯	◯	◯	◯	◯	◯
Acquire and practice skills	◯	◯	◯	◯	◯	◯	◯
Do worthwhile things	◯	◯	◯	◯	◯	◯	◯

For the MBA students, the questions were similar, although (again) referencing their last job before coming to the MBA program and, in Question 13, asking only about their peers at that job.

Responses Concerning the Eight Categories of Motivational Tools

Responses to the first two parts of the survey (except for the answers to Question 9) were provided in Tables 1 through 4 in Chapter 3. Analysis of those answers will be provided later in this appendix, but let me begin with the survey responses I gathered to the third part, concerning the eight categories of motivator. Tables A1 and A2 provide percentages of each response (for instance, from Table A1, 9.2% of the SEP participants who responded said that benefits had a powerful impact on themselves, while 18.4% said that benefits had a powerful impact on their direct reports). Using the numerical scoring system of no impact = 1, negligible impact = 2, and so on, the mean scores and standard deviations are also given in these two tables.

There is a lot going on in these data, but to take the highlights:

- Neither the SEP participants nor the MBA students come close to agreement on the impact of these categories of motivator. Every one of the eight categories has at least one participant in each group saying it has moderate impact or less, and every one has at least one participant saying that it has powerful impact or more.

Table A1. Responses of SEP Participants Concerning the Eight Categories

(a) Impact on self

	Benefits	Feeling good	Learn & grow	Pay	Praise	Job security	Acquire skills	Worthwhile things
No impact	2.4%	0.0%	0.0%	0.0%	0.0%	1.4%	0.0%	0.0%
Negligible impact	9.7%	0.0%	0.0%	1.0%	1.9%	10.6%	0.5%	1.4%
Limited impact	21.7%	1.0%	0.0%	4.3%	4.8%	23.2%	2.9%	3.4%
Moderate impact	37.2%	7.7%	7.7%	27.5%	22.2%	37.2%	22.2%	16.9%
Substantial impact	19.8%	39.6%	36.2%	37.7%	37.2%	18.4%	43.0%	32.9%
Powerful impact	9.2%	48.3%	49.8%	28.5%	30.9%	8.7%	28.5%	40.1%
I live and die …	0.0%	3.4%	6.3%	1.0%	2.9%	0.5%	2.9%	5.3%
Mean	3.90	5.45	5.55	4.91	4.99	3.88	5.05	5.23
Standard deviation	1.17	0.73	0.73	0.92	1.01	1.16	0.88	1.00

(b) Impact on peers & direct reports

	Benefits	Feeling good	Learn & grow	Pay	Praise	Job security	Acquire skills	Worthwhile things
No impact	0.5%	0.0%	0.0%	0.0%	0.0%	0.0%	0.0%	0.5%
Negligible impact	5.3%	0.0%	0.0%	0.5%	0.5%	1.0%	0.5%	0.5%
Limited impact	15.5%	1.4%	3.4%	1.4%	1.4%	8.7%	4.3%	11.6%
Moderate impact	33.8%	20.8%	22.2%	19.8%	13.0%	33.3%	25.6%	23.7%
Substantial impact	26.1%	46.9%	43.0%	41.1%	51.7%	38.6%	47.8%	40.6%
Powerful impact	18.4%	30.0%	30.0%	35.7%	31.9%	18.4%	21.3%	21.7%
They live and die …	0.5%	1.0%	1.4%	1.4%	1.4%	0.0%	0.5%	1.4%
Mean	4.37	5.08	5.04	5.14	5.17	4.65	4.86	4.74
Standard deviation	1.15	0.77	0.84	0.83	0.76	0.91	0.83	1.02

Table A2. Responses of MBA-Student Respondents Concerning the Eight Categories

(a) Impact on self

	Benefits	Feeling good	Learn & grow	Pay	Praise	Job security	Acquire skills	Worthwhile things
No impact	7.9%	0.0%	0.0%	1.3%	0.0%	3.8%	0.0%	1.3%
Negligible impact	17.5%	0.4%	0.0%	2.1%	0.4%	12.1%	0.0%	2.5%
Limited impact	22.9%	1.3%	1.3%	10.0%	3.8%	27.9%	4.2%	3.8%
Moderate impact	26.7%	11.7%	5.8%	28.3%	17.1%	31.3%	19.6%	13.8%
Substantial impact	18.8%	37.1%	29.2%	36.7%	33.8%	18.3%	39.2%	31.7%
Powerful impact	6.3%	44.6%	53.3%	21.7%	40.4%	6.3%	34.6%	38.3%
I live and die . . .	0.0%	5.0%	10.4%	0.0%	4.6%	0.4%	2.5%	8.8%
Mean	3.50	5.39	5.66	4.62	5.24	3.69	5.12	5.22
Standard deviation	1.35	0.83	0.79	1.07	0.94	1.21	0.89	1.18

(b) Impact on peers

	Benefits	Feeling good	Learn & grow	Pay	Praise	Job security	Acquire skills	Worthwhile things
No impact	5.0%	0.4%	0.0%	0.8%	0.0%	0.8%	0.0%	2.1%
Negligible impact	11.3%	0.0%	1.3%	0.8%	0.0%	3.8%	1.3%	2.1%
Limited impact	15.8%	2.5%	3.8%	5.4%	3.8%	18.8%	7.5%	9.6%
Moderate impact	25.8%	28.8%	22.1%	19.6%	18.8%	24.2%	27.5%	26.3%
Substantial impact	23.3%	40.8%	43.3%	30.0%	43.3%	29.6%	42.5%	34.2%
Powerful impact	17.9%	25.8%	27.5%	40.4%	32.9%	21.7%	20.4%	24.6%
They live and die . . .	0.8%	1.7%	2.1%	2.9%	1.3%	1.3%	0.4%	1.3%
Mean	4.08	4.94	4.98	5.10	5.09	4.48	4.75	4.67
Standard deviation	1.44	0.88	0.92	1.06	0.84	1.21	0.92	1.16

And this is not only a matter of extreme opinions; one indication of this is that the standard deviations are all in the neighborhood of a full point; other indications of this follow.

- Looking at the mean or average scores, the SEP participants give, for themselves, the highest average score to "learn and grow," then (in order) "feeling good," "doing worthwhile things," "acquire and practice skills," "praise," and "pay," with "benefits" and "job security" very far off the pace. But for their peers and direct reports, they have "praise" in first place, "pay" very close behind, "feeling good" and "learn and grow" next, then "acquire and practice skills," and "doing worthwhile things." "Benefits" trails badly, but "job security" comes very close to "worthwhile things."

    And for the MBA students, "learn and grow" is first for themselves, then "feeling good," "praise," "worthwhile things," "acquire skills," "pay," "job security," and "benefits," in that order. While for their peers, "pay" is first, then "praise," "learn and grow," "feeling good," "acquire skills," "worthwhile things," "job security" (not far from "worthwhile things"), and "benefits," in that order.

Partition these eight categories into two groups: the group of more *extrinsic* motivators—consisting of "pay," "praise," "benefits," and "job security"—and the group of motivators that are more *intrinsic*—"feeling good," "learning and growing," "acquiring and practicing skills," and "doing worthwhile things." This division isn't perfect, in the sense that (for instance) "acquisition of skills" or "learning and growing" might be instrumental for (later) receiving better extrinsic rewards (such as a promotion). But, taken with an appropriate-sized grain of salt, this division provides the following insights.

- On average, when giving opinions about the impact the motivator has on oneself, the SEP participants score each of the intrinsic group higher than each of the extrinsic group *on average*. The MBA students follow this pattern with one exception: They think (on average) that "praise" has more impact on them than "acquiring and practicing skills" and "doing worthwhile things".

- But when it comes to their peers and direct reports, the relative positions of the mean scores of different categories mix between the intrinsic and extrinsic groups.

- And compare how the SEP participants rate each category for themselves versus their peers and direct reports. In four cases—the four extrinsic motivators—the mean scores are higher for their peers than for themselves. And in the other four cases—the four intrinsics—the mean scores are higher for themselves. For the MBA students, again "praise" is the outlier: They rate it (praise) as having more impact on themselves, on average, than on their former peers.

Table A3. Average Scores for the Eight Types of Motivator

		SEP participants		MBA students	
		Average for self	Average for direct reports	Average for self	Average for direct reports
Extrinsics	Benefits	3.90	4.27	3.50	4.08
	Pay	4.91	5.14	4.62	5.10
	Praise	4.99	5.17	5.24	5.09
	Job security	3.88	4.65	3.69	4.48
Intrinsics	Feeling good	5.45	5.08	5.39	4.94
	Learn & grow	5.55	5.04	5.66	4.98
	Acquire skills	5.05	4.86	5.12	4.75
	Worthwhile things	5.23	4.74	5.22	4.67

We reprise Table 5 from the text as Table A3 here, so you can see these three points more easily. But, as you ponder these points, please be careful how you interpret them: These are statements about the average ratings given to the eight categories. It is most certainly *not* the case that all the SEP participants agree with these rankings.

For instance, the average score given by SEP participants for "pay" was 4.91, while "doing worthwhile things" averaged 5.23. As averages go, the difference is statistically significant: Resorting to statistical jargon, a paired-sample test of difference of means of the two sets of scores gives a one-tailed critical p-value of 0.00109. This means: If the population of executives (of the sort who choose to attend SEP) had equal average scores for these two, the chances that a random sample of 207 (the sample we have, to the extent that it is a random sample) would show a difference in means this large is around 1 in 1,000. (Since this is a one-sided critical p, I should say, "this large and in this direction.") In the realm of social science research, it is typical to regard any difference that gives a critical p-value smaller than 0.05 as statistically significant. So this difference is, by usual standards, very significant.*

Nonetheless in our sample of 207 executives, 55 (or 26.6%) gave a higher score to "pay" than to "worthwhile activities," and another 59 (28.5%) gave them equal scores. *Even though the average score of "worthwhile things" was very significantly greater than that of pay, over half the respondents scored pay as having equal or greater impact on them than "worthwhile things."*

Or to take the most extreme example possible: Compute two numbers for each SEP respondent: the sum of the four scores he/she gives to the four intrinsics, and the sum of the four scores he/she gives to the four extrinsics. The average over the 207 SEP respondents of the first sum of four is 21.28. The average for the second is 17.69. A difference-of-means test comparing these two sets of scores (paired-sample) gives a critical p-value (one-sided) of 1.56×10^{-35}. (This is as computed by Excel and should not be taken seriously. But the critical p-value is really, really, really small.) And yet, 21 respondents out of the 207 gave a higher sum of four to the extrinsics than to the intrinsics, with a further 15 giving equal sums. The moral here is that there is a lot of disagreement within the sample of respondents on the relative impact of these categories.

This is *not* a case in which the "majority" or average opinion is correct and those who hold contrary opinions are wrong. The

---

* The smallest difference for the SEP participants, for themselves, is between praise, at 4.99, and acquiring skills, at 5.05. This difference is not statistically significant; the critical p-values (paired-sample, one-sided) is 0.26. Next smallest is pay versus acquiring skills; the critical p-value for this comparison is 0.062.

survey asks *How strong are these motivators on* you? and . . . *on* your *peers and direct reports?* Even if the majority of people prefer apples to oranges, that doesn't make someone who prefers oranges wrong in any sense. And, as I'll later explain, there are good reasons to believe that, if (say) pay is a strong motivator for a particular respondent, it is more likely to be a strong motivator for his or her peers and direct reports. We can conclude: *There is no best way to motivate*, in the sense that it is best for everyone, in every situation and/or in every location/industry/ function/organization. You may not have needed this survey to come to that conclusion. But the data are certainly supportive.

But, granting that this is true, it becomes legitimate to ask: *What (if anything) can be learned from the* average *scores?* I think the most important lesson emerges if we first address the question, *What accounts for the difference in the average scores the participants gave the eight categories for themselves versus for their peers and direct reports?* Let me remind you what we saw in this regard in the data:

- In four cases—the four extrinsic motivators—the mean scores given by SEP participants are higher for their peers than for themselves. And in the other four cases— the four intrinsics—the mean scores are higher for themselves. For the MBA students, this pattern holds except for "praise," which the MBA respondents rate (on average) as having more impact on themselves than on their former peers.

How significant are these differences? See Table A4. First for the SEP participants and then for the MBA students, we give

Table A4. Critical p-Values for Differences in Means—Self versus Other

	SEP respondents	MBA respondents
Benefits	2.64E-13	1.24E-17
Feel good	1.92E-12	9.89E-16
Learn & grow	1.87E-15	8.78E-22
Pay	4.63E-06	1.32E-15
Praise	2.53E-03	1.08E-02
Job security	1.43E-19	1.08E-18
Skills	1.08E-03	5.09E-08
Worthwhile things	3.32E-14	1.55E-14

(paired-sample, one-tailed) critical p-values for the differences we see between average scores for self and then for peers/direct reports. Read this table together with Table A3: The SEP respondents average 3.90 for themselves for "benefits" and 4.27 for their peers and direct reports, and the critical p-value for this difference in means is 2.64×10^{-13}. (The table uses scientific notation: 2.64E-13 means 2.64×10^{-13}.) The p-values are all extraordinary small; the only p-value that is even close to the edge of (non)significance is "praise" for the MBA students, with a critical p of 0.0108. And remember, praise is the one "anomalous" category, in the sense that the SEP respondents gave a higher score to "praise" for their peers/direct reports than to themselves, while the MBA students on average scored "praise" higher for themselves.

This particular empirical finding—that people (on average) rate the extrinsic motivators as having more impact on their associates than on themselves, while they rate the four intrinsic motivators as having more impact on themselves—with differences in means that are between very and ridiculously statistically significant—is one that has recurred every year in the twelve years that I've administered this survey to SEP participants. With the exception of praise, I've found this every time I've surveyed MBA students. It has been found in every survey of every other group of executives at the Stanford GSB executive-education program that I've done. It was found in the original research on this topic by Chip Heath. Indeed, I believe that it is so likely to be true of any randomly selected (sizeable) group of managers, drawn from virtually any population of managers, that I would offer extremely good odds on a bet that it turns out to be true in any specific case. The question is, why?

To expand on what was said on this score in Chapter 5: I've asked the *Why?* question of the different groups I've surveyed, giving them the option of defending one of four possible "truths." (I'll phrase the four in terms of the SEP participants):

1. The opinions expressed by the SEP participants in both halves of this part of the survey are correct. On average, they themselves are more motivated by the intrinsic motivators than by the extrinsic motivators; their peers and direct reports present more of a mixed picture in this regard; and the participants themselves are more motivated by the intrinsic motivators and less by the extrinsic motivators than are their peers and direct reports.

2. Their opinions about themselves are largely correct, but they are wrong about their peers and direct reports, who

(in truth) are motivated similarly to how the respondents themselves are motivated.

3. Their opinions about themselves are flawed. They are motivated similarly to how they perceive their peers and direct reports are motivated.

4. The SEP participants overestimate the power of intrinsic motivators on themselves and the power of the extrinsic motivators on their peers. They underestimate the power of the extrinsic motivators on themselves and the power of the intrinsic motivators on their peers and direct reports. In other words, they are wrong in both halves of this part of the survey; the truth lies somewhere between the two.

The SEP participants, confronted with these data, have been split over which of these four possible truths is in fact the truth.

1. Some maintain that Possible Truth #1 is true, asserting that, because their direct reports are younger, less senior in their organizations, and less well-to-do, those direct reports are naturally more concerned with things like pay than are the participants themselves. If this explanation were correct, however, I should see the same effect within the data, when I look at average scores by age or rank. That is, the younger participants and those lower in their organizational ranks should be more extrinsically motivated than those who are older and higher in

rank, with the reverse true for the intrinsic categories. I'll present those data in a bit, but to deal with this now: while the data are somewhat consistent with this general idea in the case of pay, it doesn't hold up for any of the other seven categories (and it isn't all that pronounced for pay).

A more subtle argument in favor of Possible Truth #1—and one that I believe—is that the SEP participants, *because they chose to attend SEP,* are a self-selected and different-from-the-norm group of managers. In particular, their choice to attend the SEP—even given the wonderful climate of Stanford and the very nice creature comforts offered by the program—is consistent with a personal preference for learning and growing. It is not surprising, therefore, that they rate "learning and growing" highest of all, on average, and (more tenuously) they are probably individuals more likely to be motivated by other intrinsic factors. One can tell a similar story about my other surveys of SEP participants and MBA students. However, this "self-selected" character of the survey group is not present in the more carefully conducted research of Heath—indeed, Heath deals with populations in which the second set of questions is about peers only—and gets the same basic results. So, while this may explain some of what we see in the data, I don't think it is the full or primary explanation.

2. The argument most often advanced by those who defend Possible Truth #2 as true involves *availability bias.*

When dealing with their direct reports, SEP participants are more likely to discuss more tangible motivators
such as pay and benefits and job security. It goes without
saying that they are more likely to observe the impact of
praise they offer their direct reports. And they are less
likely to discuss how worthwhile is the work being done,
and so forth. So, this argument goes, assessments of the
power of the extrinsic motivators on direct reports are
too high and those of the power of intrinsic motivators
are too low. The participants have a better (fuller) sense
of what motivates themselves; that's where the truth can
be found.

3. Advocates for Possible Truth #3 advance the theory that
   most people, at some level or another, like to think of
   themselves as "better" or "more noble" than is in fact the
   case. The participants, falling victim to this bias in self-
   perception, overestimate the power of intrinsic motivators and underestimate the power of extrinsic motivators
   on themselves. The truth is found in the panels b of the
   two tables.

4. As for adherents to Possible Truth #4, they say there is
   merit in all these arguments, and the true state of affairs
   lies somewhere in the middle.

To decide definitively among these four possible truths
requires field data about the actual power of these different motivators, field data that are, for the most part, unavailable. But my

experiences and instincts, and those of others with whom I've discussed the matter, is that while Possible Truth #2 may not be true in all respects, it is certainly true that most managers underestimate the power of intrinsic motivators.* I can't say that the surveys prove anything, but *my* basic takeaways from this portion of the survey are:

- When it comes to the power of the eight categories of motivator, there is no strong consensus. Different managers are motivated differentially by the different categories.

- But, on average, there is more power and impact in intrinsic motivation for your employees than you may at first believe.

I have been *assuming* that the division into "four intrinsics" and "four extrinsics" makes sense. Certainly, this division is supported by the data in Tables A3 and A4 and, in particular (and with the exception of "praise" for MBA students), the reversal of average impact between self and others that we see in surveys, in literally all cases of which I know.

But is there more than this? In particular, are individuals either "more intrinsically motivated" or "more extrinsically" motivated? Can we divide respondents into one of two buckets of this sort? Evidence in favor (or not) of this hypothesis can be gathered

---

* The title of Chip Heath's original article on the subject, "Lay Theories of Motivation Overemphasize Extrinsic Incentives," clearly indicates that he holds this view.

by looking at the correlations in scores between pairs of the eight categories. See Table A5. This provides, first for the SEP participants and then the MBA students, the cross-category correlations on the scores they gave for themselves.

The eight categories are ordered so that the four extrinsics are first, and then the four intrinsics. The hypothesis that individuals are either "intrinsic" or "extrinsic" in orientation would be supported if we saw larger correlations in the upper-left and lower-right "triangles" and smaller or even negative correlations

Table A5. Correlations in Self-Impact Scores of the Eight Types of Motivator

(a) SEP participants

	Job security	Pay	Praise	Feeling good	Learning & growing	Skills	Worthwhile things
Benefits	0.334	0.416	0.228	0.28	0.082	0.065	0.036
Job security		0.239	0.296	0.102	0.092	0.199	0.114
Pay			0.222	0.196	0.092	0.035	-0.141
Praise				0.257	-0.019	0.049	-0.065
Feeling good					0.244	0.207	0.124
Learning & growing						0.644	0.242
Skills							0.376

(b) MBA students

	Job security	Pay	Praise	Feeling good	Learning & growing	Skills	Worthwhile things
Benefits	0.326	0.352	0.081	0.101	0.154	0.086	0.072
Job security		0.319	0.334	0.174	0.06	0.233	0.07
Pay			0.283	-0.114	0.039	0.037	-0.247
Praise				0.174	-0.002	0.051	-0.088
Feeling good					0.266	0.151	0.288
Learning & growing						0.535	0.286
Skills							0.304

in the upper-right square. And we certainly see a tendency in that direction, although there are some anomalies.*

There is more to say about the eight-category portion of the survey but, first, we should catch up on the five-channel portion.

Five Motivational Channels

In the second part of the survey, respondents were asked about five motivational channels: personal, tangible rewards; personal, intangible rewards; work that is interesting or exciting; work leading to success of the organization or workgroup; and work that is socially important. For both themselves and others, they were asked to assess the effectiveness of each channel and to say which channel was most descriptive in eliciting best work or consummate effort where, for SEP participants, the "others" were their direct reports and, for the MBA students, it was their peers on their last job. Results are provided in Tables 2 and 4 in Chapter 3 (on pages 62 and 65), and repeated in Chapter 8. (The means and standard deviations reported are computed based on the numerical scale in which not at all effective = 1, of limited effectiveness = 2, and so forth.)

---

* In both populations, job security has "high" correlation with skills. Perhaps respondents think that building their skills enhances their job security. And for the MBA students, "feeling good" and "praise" have relatively high correlation. Perhaps MBA students look for praise from external sources because they need external validation for how they are doing.

It is worth observing, perhaps, that *all* the correlations tend to be positive, if not hugely so. This reflects a "scaling" individual-fixed effect: Some people are more likely to use the right-hand scale options; others the left-hand scale options.

In terms of motivating others, respondents were asked Question 9, concerning how similar their direct reports or peers were in terms of motivation. The distributions of answers to this question for the two groups are provided in Table A6.

Just as in the other part of the survey, there is a lot going on in these data. Some highlights are:

- As before, no consensus emerges. The respondents do not, for the most part, agree. This is perhaps most obvious if you look at the data for which of the five channels is most descriptive: The highest percentage for any of the five channels is "interesting work," for the MBA students themselves, at 37.9%; this channel also scores high in the other three cases, but not quite as high as "organizational success" for the SEP participants. At

Table A6. Survey Responses to Questions about the Five Motivational Channels.

(a) SEP participants

Direct reports are quite different. To motivate their best work, I must vary the techniques used:	58.9%
Direct reports are different, but they can be (and are) motivated in largely similar ways:	35.7%
Direct reports are very similar in how to motivate them, and I treat them similarly, accordingly:	5.3%

(b) MBA students

Peers were quite different. To motivate their best work, different techniques were necessary	29.2%
Peers were different, but they could be motivated in largely similar ways:	51.7%
Peers were very similar in terms of motivation, and were treated similarly, accordingly:	19.2%

the other end of the spectrum, the smallest percentage for most descriptive by the SEP participants is still over 10% ("praise," for self), while for the MBA students, it is 4.6% ("organizational success," peers).

- This variety in answers is buttressed by the fact that, for the SEP respondents, nearly 60% say that their direct reports are so different that motivational techniques must be tailored to the individuals. Contrast this with the 70% of MBA students who say that similar motivational techniques work for their peers, even though they perceive substantial difference in what motivates those peers.

- "Interesting and/or exciting work" is the all-around winner. It has the highest mean score in all four cases. Even more impressively, over 94% of the SEP participants see it as very effective or better for themselves, while over 93% see it as very effective or better for their direct reports, over 93% of the MBA students see it as very effective or better for themselves, and 89% of the MBA students see it as very effective or better for their peers. As discussed in the text, "interesting and/or exciting work" is the motivational magic bullet, *if* what your employees find interesting and exciting in their work is what you want them to do.

- The tangible-rewards channel does not do poorly, but in terms of average scores, it lags in all four cases behind "interesting and exciting work" and "praise." And, for the SEP respondents, it ranks below organizational success both for self and for direct reports. The percentage of respondents saying it is most descriptive is below 20% for all but the MBA students, concerning their peers. If the message from the eight-category part of the survey is that people may underestimate the power of intrinsic motivators (at least, on others) and overestimate the relative power of extrinsic motivators (praise excepted), this message is being reinforced here.

- "Praise" does fairly well, and is particularly effective with the MBA students, or so they say.

- "Success of the organization" does very well with the SEP respondents, especially for themselves. This is enhanced by a strong demographic effect: For the sub-sample of respondents who are chairs/CEOs/managing partners/presidents, "success of the organization" has an average score of 4.86, while for COOs the average score is 4.67. (These compare with an average score of 4.50 for the remainder of the population; in a difference-of-means test comparing the average scores for CEOs and COOs versus all the others, with assumed equal variance, the critical p (one-sided) is 0.0032.) Apparently, people put in a position of responsibility for an organization tend to take to heart responsibility for that organization's success. On the other hand, the MBA respondents both for themselves and their peers give "organizational success" pretty low average marks (relative to the others), and "organizational success," for them, comes a pretty poor fifth place in terms of what is most descriptive. (A more detailed comparison of the MBA students versus the SEP participants, is presented later.)

- "Socially important work" does relatively poorly in mean scores, coming in last place in all four cases. But, for over one in ten MBA students, it is most descriptive, rising to nearly one in eight among the SEP participants for their direct reports and over one in five for themselves.

Table A7 provides a comparison of each group's average score for self versus the other in their sample, together with critical p-values. The SEP participants give higher average scores for themselves than for their direct reports for all five channels—perhaps they feel that they have a hard time motivating those

Table A7. Five-Channel Average Scores Comparisons: Self versus Other

(a) SEP participants

	Pay, etc.	Praise, etc.	Work	Org success	Social good
Self average	3.85	4.15	4.66	4.58	3.78
Direct reports average	3.77	4.06	4.51	4.07	3.32
Critical p	0.10	0.09	2.12E-03	2.44E-16	7.52E-13

(b) MBA Students

	Pay, etc.	Praise, etc.	Work	Org success	Social good
Self average	3.88	4.43	4.73	3.61	3.60
Peers average	4.06	4.25	4.45	3.32	3.14
Critical p	2.88E-04	2.68E-04	6.81E-06	9.98E-06	2.01E-12

direct reports—but the differences are most pronounced (and significant) for organizational success and social good. The MBA students are roughly similar, except that they give a higher average score to their peers than to themselves for "pay." The most pronounced difference is for "social good," although for the MBA students, all the differences meet the usual test of statistical significance in social science. But, to reiterate from before, this concerns average scores; there are appreciable numbers of both SEP participants and MBA students whose scores go in the other directions.

And Table A8 provides data on the between-channel correlations, for both the SEP participants and the MBA students. In this case (unlike the eight-categories case), there is no special "grouping" of the channels, which is largely borne out by Table A8; most of the correlations are slightly positive or slightly neg-

Table A8. Between-Channel Correlations on Self-Impact Scores

(a) SEP participants

	Praise, etc.	Work	Org success	Social good
Pay, etc.	0.233	0.131	-0.002	-0.072
Praise, etc.		0.143	0.122	0.086
Work			0.196	0.139
Org success				0.168

(b) MBA students

	Praise, etc.	Work	Org success	Social good
Pay, etc.	0.200	-0.017	-0.052	-0.164
Praise, etc.		0.003	0.072	-0.085
Work			0.045	0.106
Org success				0.435

ative. The most glaring exception is strong positive correlation between "organizational success" and "social good" for the MBA students; perhaps for those students who worked for social-purpose organizations, success of the organization means contributing to the social good. In both samples, we also see mild positive correlation between "pay" and "praise"; perhaps this reflects a distinction between individuals who are more extrinsically motivated and those with more of an intrinsic motivation.

Explaining the Variety of Answers, I: Demography?

Why are different managers differentially impacted by these eight categories? Why are the five channels differentially effective? *What underlying factors account for these differences?*

Demography might explain some of the differences. Consider, for instance, the following stereotype-based hypotheses:

- European managers are less motivated by money (on average) than are managers from the United States and Canada.

- People in the financial services industries are also more motivated by money than are, say, managers drawn from the population as a whole.

- On average, praise has greater impact on women than on men.

(Before reading further, what is your guess as to the truth of these hypotheses? Do you have other, similar hypotheses that you believe to be true?)

To test these and similar hypotheses, in Table A9, I present the average scores given by various subsets of the SEP participants for themselves and, in some cases, for their peers/direct reports.

- I only present results for one demographic category at a time. That is, I give the average scores for Europeans, and I give the average scores for participants who are between 40 and 44 years old, but I do not give results for Europeans who are between 40 and 44 years old.

- I do not give results from groups smaller than six individuals.

- Consistent with those two rules, I give average self-scores broken down by home base, age, sex, organizational rank, functional specialty, and industry. But for average scores for direct reports, I only give home base, functional specialty, and industry; since age, sex and, to a lesser extent, rank of the respondent don't tell you the demographic characteristics of the respondent's direct reports.

Please do not overprocess these numbers. The sizes of the various groups are such that statistical significance is rare.* My take on

---

* If you want to engage in testing statistical significance for any specific hypotheses you might have, and if you know how, be my guest. It is probably reasonable to run such tests with an assumed equal standard deviation of 1 for each underlying population.

Table A9. SEP Average Scores by Demographic Groups

(a) Self-scores

	N	Benefits	Feeling good	Learn & grow	Pay	Praise	Job security
Home base							
US/Canada	62	3.58	5.40	5.63	4.98	4.82	3.77
Latin America	10	3.90	5.10	5.30	4.90	4.80	4.00
Europe	58	3.97	5.48	5.57	4.76	5.07	3.78
East/South Asia	46	4.28	5.54	5.50	5.00	5.26	4.24
Middle East/Africa	6	3.67	5.50	5.17	4.67	4.67	3.50
Australia/NZ/Pacific Islands	25	3.88	5.48	5.56	5.00	4.88	3.80
Age							
Less than 40	34	3.76	5.47	5.71	5.32	4.94	3.62
40 to 44	69	3.94	5.54	5.67	4.86	4.93	3.78
45 to 49	64	4.03	5.41	5.39	4.91	5.00	3.94
50 to 54	30	3.67	5.40	5.57	4.67	5.00	4.03
55 and older	10	3.90	5.30	5.10	4.70	5.50	4.70
Sex							
Male	178	3.92	5.42	5.53	4.93	4.98	3.83
Female	29	3.76	5.69	5.62	4.79	5.07	4.21
Rank							
Chair/CEO/managing partner/president	44	3.75	5.45	5.45	4.75	4.75	3.68
COO	9	3.78	5.33	5.33	4.11	4.22	3.78
Head of staff function—CFO, etc.	40	3.70	5.45	5.60	4.98	5.23	3.83
Senior VP/partner	23	4.26	5.39	5.61	4.96	5.17	4.09
VP/partner	40	3.83	5.50	5.80	4.93	5.03	3.90
General manager	51	4.10	5.47	5.39	5.12	5.04	4.02
Functional Specialty							
General management	94	4.05	5.51	5.54	4.93	5.03	3.86
Finance	19	4.16	5.53	5.63	5.26	5.21	3.95
Accounting	1						
Marketing	15	3.27	5.53	5.53	4.87	5.00	4.07
Prod./ops./mfg.	13	3.23	5.15	5.77	4.92	4.92	3.62
Information technology	17	3.35	5.12	5.29	4.47	4.59	3.12
Human resource management	4						
Strategic planning	12	3.67	5.67	5.33	4.83	5.33	4.08
Other	32	4.13	5.47	5.63	4.88	4.84	4.22
Industry							
Financial services/investments	37	3.97	5.59	5.65	5.16	4.86	3.86
IT/electronics/computers	48	3.69	5.31	5.63	4.67	4.81	3.42
Manufacturing/construction	30	3.60	5.47	5.37	5.07	5.27	3.90
Health care/pharma/biotech	16	3.88	5.44	5.63	4.63	4.69	4.19
Marketing/retail	13	3.77	5.54	5.69	5.00	5.54	4.15
Public sector	12	4.42	5.42	5.33	4.75	5.17	4.58
Consulting/advisory/education	11	4.27	5.82	5.73	4.91	4.91	3.55
Other	40	4.10	5.38	5.43	5.00	5.03	4.13

Acquire & practice skills	Do worthwhile things	Pay, etc.	Praise, etc.	Interesting & exciting work	Organizational success	Social contribution
			Five channels			
5.05	5.24	4.05	4.05	4.63	4.55	3.69
4.70	5.20	3.50	4.00	4.50	4.60	3.70
5.22	5.34	3.57	4.12	4.81	4.52	3.52
4.91	5.20	3.85	4.35	4.43	4.67	4.20
4.67	5.33	3.83	4.33	4.50	4.50	3.50
5.12	4.96	4.12	4.16	4.92	4.68	3.96
5.29	5.15	4.18	4.21	4.82	4.56	3.62
5.07	5.29	3.80	4.10	4.67	4.48	3.75
4.88	5.16	3.80	4.06	4.56	4.63	3.77
5.17	5.20	3.80	4.37	4.67	4.63	3.83
4.80	5.60	3.50	4.30	4.70	5.00	4.50
5.02	5.22	3.84	4.14	4.65	4.60	3.74
5.21	5.28	3.90	4.24	4.76	4.52	4.07
4.89	5.34	3.91	4.05	4.73	4.86	4.09
4.67	5.00	3.56	3.89	4.56	4.67	3.67
5.20	5.10	3.73	4.38	4.70	4.58	3.53
5.00	5.52	3.91	4.35	4.65	4.43	4.00
5.33	5.18	3.83	4.08	4.63	4.60	3.45
4.94	5.18	3.92	4.10	4.63	4.39	3.90
5.04	5.27	4.00	4.14	4.69	4.67	3.88
5.00	5.21	3.74	4.47	4.74	4.42	3.53
5.27	5.27	3.67	3.73	4.87	4.67	3.53
5.08	4.92	3.46	4.08	4.85	4.92	3.62
4.76	5.29	3.53	3.88	4.12	4.71	3.47
4.58	5.00	3.83	4.33	4.58	4.33	3.75
5.28	5.19	3.75	4.31	4.69	4.34	3.88
5.08	5.35	4.11	4.16	4.97	4.49	3.81
4.94	5.19	3.81	4.06	4.48	4.71	3.77
4.97	5.23	3.87	4.17	4.63	4.47	3.27
5.38	5.06	3.63	4.06	4.81	4.38	3.88
5.23	4.92	3.77	4.31	4.85	5.00	3.54
5.17	5.50	3.42	4.50	4.58	4.42	4.58
5.27	5.64	4.00	4.27	4.73	4.36	4.09
4.93	5.13	3.83	4.10	4.50	4.68	3.88

(continued)

Table A9 (continued)

				(b) Scores for peers/direct reports			
			Eight categories				
	N	Benefits	Feeling good	Learn & grow	Pay	Praise	Job security
Home base							
US/Canada	62	4.08	4.85	5.03	5.15	5.15	4.65
Latin America	10	4.10	5.10	5.10	5.20	5.30	4.50
Europe	58	4.47	5.26	5.14	5.02	5.19	4.66
East/South Asia	46	4.80	5.20	5.02	5.28	5.20	4.72
Middle East/Africa	6	4.67	4.83	4.33	5.50	5.17	4.50
Australia/NZ/Pacific Islands	25	4.08	5.08	5.00	5.08	5.12	4.60
Functional specialty							
General management	94	4.51	5.13	5.05	5.14	5.20	4.70
Finance	19	4.58	5.05	5.00	5.26	5.26	4.68
Accounting	1						
Marketing	15	4.13	5.20	5.00	4.93	5.13	4.60
Prod./ops./mfg.	13	3.85	4.62	5.31	5.08	5.23	4.38
Information technology	17	3.88	4.88	4.76	4.88	4.88	4.06
Human resource management	4						
Strategic planning	12	3.83	5.08	4.75	5.17	5.08	4.33
Other	32	4.59	5.16	5.16	5.34	5.19	4.91
Industry							
Financial services/investments	37	4.51	5.22	4.86	5.43	5.00	4.73
IT/electronics/computers	48	4.13	5.02	5.25	5.08	5.31	4.50
Manufacturing/construction	30	4.27	4.93	5.13	5.03	5.27	4.53
Health care/pharma/biotech	16	4.19	4.88	5.19	4.75	4.63	4.50
Marketing/retail	13	4.31	5.15	5.00	5.23	5.85	4.92
Public sector	12	4.75	5.08	4.75	5.25	5.08	5.00
Consulting/advisory/education	11	4.82	5.36	5.00	5.36	5.27	4.82
Other	40	4.45	5.13	4.93	5.08	5.10	4.65

what is significant in these numbers—and I mean significant in terms of the magnitude of the effects as much as their statistical significance—are: (a) None of these categories explains a lot. People in different demographic groups give responses that are more alike, in general, than they are different. (b) People in the public sector, however, are a lot more motivated by social contribution and by benefits than are other groups. (c) Chairs/CEOs and, to a somewhat lesser extent, COOs, give higher scores to themselves in terms of motivation by the success of their orga-

Acquire & practice skills	Do worthwhile things	Five channels				
		Pay, etc.	Praise, etc.	Interesting & exciting work	Organizational success	Social contribution
4.79	4.63	3.84	4.21	4.61	4.26	3.19
4.60	4.80	3.30	3.40	4.00	3.90	3.30
5.03	4.90	3.59	4.07	4.76	4.02	3.40
4.85	4.78	3.91	3.98	4.13	3.87	3.39
4.83	5.00	4.17	3.67	4.00	4.17	2.67
4.80	4.52	3.84	4.20	4.72	4.16	3.48
4.87	4.81	3.87	4.11	4.54	4.17	3.36
4.68	4.95	3.68	3.79	4.21	3.63	3.37
5.07	4.67	3.47	4.13	4.73	4.27	3.07
5.15	4.54	3.54	4.15	4.69	4.15	3.15
4.53	4.65	3.76	3.94	4.41	4.24	3.35
4.50	4.33	3.42	4.00	4.33	3.83	3.08
5.00	4.69	3.84	4.09	4.53	3.97	3.28
4.78	4.92	4.03	3.84	4.59	3.92	3.19
4.90	4.67	3.65	4.04	4.56	4.27	3.35
4.93	4.77	3.73	4.20	4.53	4.00	3.10
4.75	4.56	3.88	4.25	4.63	4.06	3.25
5.23	4.54	3.38	4.62	5.00	4.31	3.31
4.83	5.25	3.58	3.92	4.08	3.92	3.92
4.82	4.91	4.09	3.91	4.45	4.09	3.64
4.80	4.60	3.75	4.03	4.30	4.00	3.33

nization. (d) People in the financial sector give themselves high average scores for pay in the eight-category portion of the survey; not so much in the five channels. But when it comes to their peers/direct reports, they certainly believe the stereotypes. And the consulting types are not far behind (especially when you consider that the consulting group mixes in at least a few academic administrators who went through the SEP, and I have a hard time thinking that academics would admit to being highly motivated by pay).

Table A10. MBA Students' Average Scores by Demographic Groups

(a) Self-scores

							Eight categories
	N	Benefits	Feeling good	Learn & grow	Pay	Praise	Job security
Geography							
US/Canada	170	3.34	5.35	5.58	4.44	5.21	3.69
Latin America	18	3.67	5.56	5.67	5.00	5.11	3.50
Europe	20	3.70	5.55	6.00	5.10	5.20	3.55
East/South Asia	17	4.71	5.47	6.06	5.24	5.41	4.06
Middle East/Africa	12	3.58	5.42	5.58	5.17	5.67	3.83
Australia/NZ/Pacific Islands (N = 3) too small a sample to give results							
Age							
25 years old or younger	32	3.66	5.28	5.53	4.75	5.22	3.69
26 to 30 years old	192	3.43	5.39	5.69	4.63	5.22	3.64
31 years or older	16	4.00	5.69	5.56	4.31	5.44	4.25
Sex							
Male	136	3.61	5.26	5.58	4.64	5.13	3.56
Female	104	3.35	5.57	5.76	4.60	5.38	3.86
Functional specialty							
General management	61	3.46	5.43	5.69	4.30	5.23	3.64
Finance	57	3.51	5.23	5.53	4.82	5.35	3.91
Marketing	20	3.95	5.10	5.55	5.15	5.20	3.85
Ops./prod./mfg.	13	3.46	5.23	5.54	4.69	5.08	3.62
Strategic planning	47	3.49	5.53	5.87	4.64	5.23	3.53
Other	33	3.45	5.55	5.52	4.58	5.21	3.61
Accounting (N = 1), Information technology (N = 3), and human resource management (N = 5) too small to give result							
Industry							
Financial services/ investments	58	3.48	5.28	5.50	4.86	5.31	3.83
IT/electronics/computer tech	25	3.80	5.56	5.76	4.72	5.36	3.76
Manufacturing/construction	10	3.50	5.40	5.60	4.90	4.80	3.60
Healthcare/pharma/biotech	19	3.47	5.37	5.68	4.68	5.32	3.47
Marketing/retail	12	3.42	5.58	5.92	4.92	5.50	4.00
Public sector	16	3.75	5.63	5.56	4.06	5.19	4.25
Consulting	49	3.37	5.31	5.71	4.67	5.31	3.59
Education	10	3.20	5.80	5.40	4.30	5.40	3.60
Not for profit/social enterprise	10	3.70	5.60	5.80	3.90	4.80	3.80
Entertainment	9	3.22	5.00	5.89	4.44	5.22	3.33
Other	20	3.50	5.35	5.65	4.45	4.90	3.40
Social media (N = 1) and student just prior (N = 1) too small to give results							
College major							
Economics	50	3.80	5.64	5.86	4.74	5.16	3.80
Business	40	3.68	5.25	5.63	4.95	5.40	3.65
Other social science	34	3.18	5.62	5.62	4.41	5.29	3.71
Engineering	51	3.47	5.29	5.63	4.61	5.22	3.16
Biological Sciences	17	3.76	5.12	5.59	4.65	5.41	4.18
Physical sciences or math	14	3.36	5.36	5.64	4.79	5.57	4.43
Humanities	34	3.12	5.26	5.53	4.21	4.91	3.79

Acquire & practice skills	Do worthwhile things	Five channels				
		Pay, etc.	Praise, etc.	Interesting & exciting work	Organizational success	Social contribution
5.05	5.21	3.79	4.37	4.70	3.60	3.61
5.11	5.22	3.83	4.28	4.89	3.39	3.83
5.45	5.10	4.20	4.40	4.90	3.45	3.20
5.53	5.41	4.41	4.71	4.76	4.29	3.82
4.92	5.33	3.83	4.92	4.83	3.25	3.50
5.00	4.94	3.84	4.31	4.72	3.34	3.44
5.12	5.23	3.89	4.46	4.74	3.61	3.61
5.31	5.63	3.75	4.31	4.69	4.06	3.88
5.04	5.13	3.89	4.32	4.76	3.56	3.45
5.21	5.34	3.86	4.57	4.70	3.67	3.81
5.25	5.36	3.79	4.39	4.80	3.69	3.75
5.09	4.68	4.07	4.49	4.61	3.44	3.02
4.90	4.90	4.10	4.30	4.40	3.70	3.55
5.38	5.62	3.69	4.08	4.77	3.92	3.54
5.19	5.38	3.91	4.53	4.87	3.55	3.96
4.73	5.39	3.58	4.36	4.70	3.52	3.79
5.10	4.66	4.14	4.53	4.64	3.43	2.97
5.40	5.36	4.12	4.32	4.64	3.84	3.44
5.20	5.20	4.10	4.10	4.60	3.50	3.70
5.32	5.74	3.63	4.53	4.84	3.74	4.05
5.58	5.33	4.00	4.42	4.75	3.92	3.00
4.94	5.69	3.88	4.13	4.94	4.31	4.31
5.18	5.06	3.80	4.67	4.80	3.41	3.69
4.40	5.80	3.40	4.60	4.50	3.80	4.70
5.20	6.10	3.40	4.20	5.00	4.20	4.80
4.78	5.11	3.78	4.22	4.44	3.78	3.00
4.75	5.45	3.55	4.05	4.85	3.15	3.90
5.16	5.18	4.04	4.54	4.76	3.84	3.66
5.05	4.93	4.05	4.50	4.65	3.38	3.20
4.88	5.38	3.59	4.68	4.59	3.56	3.85
5.18	5.31	3.84	4.22	4.82	3.47	3.45
5.29	5.59	3.94	4.59	4.94	3.41	4.06
5.14	5.00	4.00	4.14	4.64	3.57	3.57
5.18	5.24	3.68	4.29	4.74	3.91	3.76

(continued)

Table A10 *(continued)*

					(b) Scores for peers		
				Eight categories			
	N	Benefits	Feeling good	Learn & grow	Pay	Praise	Job security
Geography							
US/Canada	170	3.87	4.86	4.96	4.95	5.06	4.42
Latin America	18	4.72	5.06	5.17	5.44	5.06	4.50
Europe	20	4.40	5.25	5.20	5.30	4.90	4.60
East/South Asia	17	5.35	5.06	5.12	5.65	5.59	4.76
Middle East/Africa	12	4.08	4.83	4.75	5.58	5.08	4.75
Australia/NZ/Pacific Islands (N = 3) too small a sample to give results							
Functional specialty							
General management	61	4.05	4.90	5.03	4.85	5.08	4.44
Finance	57	3.72	4.81	4.93	5.42	5.11	4.25
Marketing	20	4.40	4.65	4.70	5.30	4.90	4.70
Ops./prod./mfg.	13	4.54	4.85	5.15	5.08	5.08	5.08
Strategic planning	47	4.30	4.89	5.06	5.11	5.23	4.45
Other	33	4.39	5.15	4.79	5.00	5.00	4.79
Accounting (N = 1), information technology (N = 3), and human resource management (N = 5) too small to give results							
Industry							
Financial services/ investments	58	3.79	4.79	4.86	5.55	5.17	4.34
IT/electronics/computer tech	25	4.28	4.92	5.24	4.96	5.20	4.72
Manufacturing/construction	10	4.70	4.70	4.90	5.50	4.70	5.70
Health care/pharma/biotech	19	4.05	4.89	5.11	5.11	5.32	4.84
Marketing/retail	12	4.50	5.17	4.67	5.50	5.25	4.92
Public sector	16	4.63	4.69	4.44	4.19	4.75	4.94
Consulting	49	3.67	5.02	5.43	4.98	5.20	3.86
Education	10	4.30	5.40	4.80	4.70	5.00	4.60
Not for profit/social enterprise	10	4.20	4.90	5.20	4.40	4.70	4.10
Entertainment	9	4.33	4.56	4.33	5.44	4.89	4.67
Other	20	4.45	5.15	4.65	5.05	4.90	4.85
Social media (N = 1) and student just prior (N = 1) too small to give results							

Concerning the MBA students, similar data are presented in Table A10. Make of these what you will.

While it is difficult to find much explanatory power from demographic groups within each of the two surveys, there are marked differences between the responses given by MBA students and SEP participants. The demographic differences between

Acquire & practice skills	Do worthwhile things	Five channels				
		Pay, etc.	Praise, etc.	Interesting & exciting work	Organizational success	Social contribution
4.73	4.73	4.02	4.28	4.54	3.31	3.15
4.83	4.89	3.83	4.06	4.94	3.50	3.56
4.90	4.10	4.30	4.10	4.60	3.25	2.75
4.65	4.41	4.59	4.24	3.94	3.59	2.94
4.50	4.75	4.08	4.42	4.08	2.92	3.25
4.80	4.79	4.10	4.46	4.64	3.39	3.28
4.86	4.23	4.33	4.21	4.33	3.30	2.53
4.65	4.10	3.95	4.15	4.35	3.20	3.00
4.46	4.77	3.77	3.92	4.15	3.38	3.23
4.81	4.94	4.04	4.23	4.45	3.26	3.53
4.42	4.94	3.79	4.09	4.61	3.18	3.27
4.79	4.00	4.41	4.34	4.31	3.22	2.48
4.80	4.80	3.92	4.08	4.60	3.20	3.00
4.30	4.20	4.20	3.70	4.00	3.50	3.00
4.95	5.21	4.11	4.37	4.42	3.37	3.47
4.50	4.08	4.33	4.17	4.25	3.75	2.75
4.81	5.38	4.13	4.25	4.69	3.69	3.94
4.86	5.06	4.00	4.43	4.76	3.20	3.31
4.50	5.40	3.40	4.50	4.70	3.40	3.90
5.00	5.60	3.50	4.20	4.70	3.60	4.70
4.67	4.22	4.00	4.11	4.56	3.56	3.11
4.20	4.50	3.85	3.95	4.45	3.10	3.10

the two populations are manifest: SEP participants are older and, in virtually all cases, highly accomplished senior managers. Stanford MBA students are considerably younger, and while they already have a record of considerable success in their careers, those careers are (so far) a good deal shorter. It perhaps isn't accurate to say that the SEP participants are what the MBA students aspire to become; Stanford MBA students are, overall, less interested in working for established companies and much more interested in starting their own, which may also account for some of the differences. In any event, Table A11 directly compares the average scores given by SEP participants and MBA students, with critical p-values for difference-of-means tests.*

The large (and statistically significant) differences are obvious. MBA students are more motivated (on average) by praise. They care less about benefits. And the biggest difference: They are much less motivated, and (if we believe the survey results) their peers are much less motivated, by success of the organization for which they work. (It stands to reason that the MBA students have less career concerns involving their *former* employer than do the SEP participants, involving their current employer. So this comparison may be a bit unfair as a test of MBA-student loyalty.)

One inexplicable result in these data concerns the motivational power of pay. In the five-channel portion of the survey, MBA students gave pay a very slightly higher average score than did the SEP participants for themselves, but a significantly higher score for the peers than the SEP participants gave for their direct reports. But in the eight-category portion, the SEP participants gave higher scores to pay than did the MBA students, both for themselves and for their "others." And the significant difference in this part of the survey was in self-scores. The moral of this anomaly may be: Most such survey results should be regarded with at least some skepticism.

---

* These tests are, of course, not paired-sample tests. I do use implied equal variance, since the standard deviations are quite similar.

Table A11. Mean-Score Comparisons: SEP Respondents versus MBA-Student Respondents

	Self scores			"Others"		
	SEP average	MBA average	critical p	SEP average	MBA average	critical p
Five channels						
Pay, etc.	3.85	3.88	0.37	3.77	4.06	3.1E-04
Praise, etc.	4.15	4.43	4.1E-04	4.06	4.25	3.2E-03
Interesting work	4.66	4.73	0.155	4.51	4.45	0.417
Organizational success	4.58	3.61	7.7E-25	4.07	3.32	1.8E-16
Social good	3.78	3.60	5.1E-02	3.32	3.14	0.037
Eight categories						
Benefits	3.90	3.50	4.7E-04	4.27	4.08	0.012
Feeling good	5.45	5.39	2.0E-01	5.08	4.94	0.038
Learning & growing	5.55	5.66	0.061	5.04	4.98	0.255
Pay	4.91	4.62	1.2E-03	5.14	5.10	0.312
Praise	4.99	5.24	3.9E-03	5.17	5.09	0.142
Job security	3.88	3.69	0.041	4.65	4.48	0.051
Acquire skills	5.05	5.12	0.209	4.86	4.75	0.084
Worthwhile things	5.23	5.22	0.476	4.74	4.67	0.242

Explaining the Variety of Answers, Part II: An Organization-Fixed Effect

The question *How effective is motivational channel X or category Y?* is best answered "It depends." And this leads to, *On what does it depend?* A short summary of the last section is, "Not on demographic variables for the most part," unless you are talking about demographic variation on the scale of MBA students versus mature managers.

So is there any affirmative answer that we can give to the *On what . . .* question? Economists and social psychologists alike would expect, at some level, to see an organization-based fixed effect: That is, employees within a given organization will tend to be motivated in similar fashion. Economists would justify this assertion based on screening mechanisms: Different organizations will offer different sorts of motivational schemes, and (prospective) employees will sort themselves, to some extent, into organizations whose screening mechanisms match their own strengths and preferences. So, for instance, we have the theory of RE/MAX described back in Chapter 2: RE/MAX has an economic incentive scheme that is designed to attract aggressive, workaholic types of agents; indeed, the business model of RE/MAX is built on this attraction. And, as Safelite observed, putting in place the PPP system changed the type of individual who signed up with and then stayed with Safelite as a technician.

And a social psychologist, while agreeing with this screening effect, would go beyond it: Individuals within an organization in which many fellow employees are motivated in one fashion or another will tend to become like those employee, through the process of self-perception and attribution.

These theoretical expectations can be tested the survey data in several ways. Most directly, respondents, in the five-channel portion of the survey, were asked, *How similar are your direct reports/ peers, in terms of motivation?* For the SEP participants, the answer was, "Not very similar"; nearly 60% of the SEP respondents said that their direct reports required individualized motivation. The MBA students, on the other hand, were more encouraging to the aforementioned theoretical speculations, with 20% saying that their peers were motivationally similar, and another 50% saying that their peers were similar enough so that the same motivational schemes would be effective.

We can also look at the correlations between answers given for self versus for "other," since in all cases the other is a member of the same organization as the self. Table A12 gives these correlations for the SEP participants, and Table A13 gives them for the MBA students. In each table, the rows are the self-scores, and the columns are the scores for the "other" in the survey.

What we would want to see to support these theories, and what we do see in the data to some extent, are large positive correlations along the diagonal of each of these correlation matrices. Some of the diagonal correlations are not as large as would be ideal from the perspective of supporting these theories, but they are all positive and the least of them in each of the four matrices is larger than any of the off-diagonal elements.

Finally, there are data in the five-channel portion of the survey on the most descriptive motivational channel. Table A14 provides the following set of statistics. For each of the five channels, the distribution of responses for the other is given conditional on the response given for the self. So, for instance, for the SEP participants, 17.4% of all respondents said that motivation of their direct report's best work by tangible personal rewards, such as pay, was most descriptive for their organization. This is from the first column. But, of the 15.5% of all respondents who said that pay was most descriptive of what motivates themselves, 40.6% (of the 15.5%) said that pay was most descriptive for their

Table A12. Correlations in Scores Given for Self (Rows) versus Others (Columns): SEP Participants.

(a) Eight categories

	Benefits	Feeling good	Learn & grow	Pay	Praise	Job security	Skills	Worthwhile
Benefits	0.72	0.22	0.14	0.39	0.10	0.31	0.08	0.12
Feeling good	0.36	0.54	0.19	0.16	0.16	0.13	0.23	0.12
Learn & grow	0.16	0.23	0.41	0.08	0.05	0.19	0.38	0.14
Pay	0.41	0.12	0.03	0.66	0.09	0.30	-0.02	-0.08
Praise	0.18	0.26	0.13	0.15	0.48	0.18	0.09	-0.04
Job security	0.22	0.07	0.08	0.20	0.12	0.46	0.15	0.11
Acquire skills	0.17	0.22	0.31	0.05	0.05	0.26	0.51	0.27
Worthwhile things	0.17	0.14	0.14	-0.12	-0.02	0.17	0.27	0.63

(b) Five channels

	Pay, etc.	Praise, etc.	Interesting work	Org. success	Social good
Pay, etc.	0.58	0.03	0.02	-0.07	-0.14
Praise, etc.	0.16	0.30	-0.08	-0.04	0.03
Interesting work	0.10	0.13	0.48	0.08	0.09
Organizational success	0.03	0.11	0.09	0.45	0.09
Social good	0.17	0.09	0.03	0.20	0.63

direct reports (second column, first row). And, looking still at the same subgroup—the 15.5% who said that pay was most descriptive for themselves—only 6.3% said that organizational success was most descriptive for their direct reports (second column, fourth row) versus 23.7% overall (first column, fourth row). Or, to take another example, 23.7% overall said that organizational success was most descriptive for their direct reports. But of the 27.5% who said that organizational success was most descriptive

Table A13. Correlations in Scores Given Self (Rows) versus Others (Columns): MBA Students

(a) Eight categories

	Benefits	Feeling good	Learn & grow	Pay	Praise	Job security	Skills	Worthwhile things
Benefits	0.75	0.13	0.12	0.30	0.15	0.34	0.11	0.05
Feeling good	0.17	0.54	0.25	0.01	0.11	0.14	0.13	0.26
Learn & grow	0.19	0.24	0.33	0.14	0.17	0.09	0.27	0.14
Pay	0.30	-0.06	0.13	0.66	0.25	0.32	0.09	-0.16
Praise	0.08	0.16	0.04	0.25	0.41	0.19	0.13	0.00
Job Security	0.25	0.16	0.16	0.25	0.25	0.43	0.21	0.20
Skills	0.06	0.26	0.30	0.04	0.14	0.08	0.35	0.18
Worthwhile things	0.13	0.33	0.19	-0.11	0.02	0.17	0.15	0.60

(b) Five channels

	Pay, etc.	Praise, etc.	Work	Organizational success	Social good
Pay, etc.	0.56	0.19	-0.02	-0.06	-0.18
Praise, etc.	-0.03	0.51	0.11	0.10	0.01
Work	-0.06	0.00	0.36	-0.07	0.11
Organizational success	-0.02	0.07	0.12	0.52	0.31
Social good	-0.12	-0.05	0.10	0.39	0.65

for themselves, 49.1% said that it was most descriptive for their direct reports. And so forth.

These numbers are certainly supportive of the theories. They aren't dispositive: other explanations for the positive correlations in Tables A12 and A13 and the conditional distributions shown in Table A14 can be offered. For instance, to the extent that people naturally believe that other people are similar to themselves, if channel X is most descriptive of what motivates one's own best

Table A14. Conditional Distributions of "Most Descriptive" Motivational Channel for the Other, Conditional on "Most Descriptive" for Self

(a) For SEP participants

	Overall	If pay is most descriptive for self	If praise is most descriptive for self	If interesting work is most descriptive	If organizational success most descriptive	If social good is most descriptive
Pay most descriptive for other	17.4%	40.6%	26.1%	7.5%	12.3%	14.3%
Praise is most descriptive	20.2%	18.8%	65.2%	7.5%	15.8%	19.0%
Interesting work is most descriptive	26.6%	25.0%	8.7%	58.5%	21.1%	4.8%
Organizational success is most descriptive	23.7%	6.3%	0.0%	20.8%	49.1%	19.0%
Social good is most descriptive	12.1%	9.4%	0.0%	5.7%	1.8%	42.9%

(b) For MBA students

	Overall	If pay is most descriptive for self	If praise is most descriptive for self	If interesting work is most descriptive	If organizational success most descriptive	If social good is most descriptive
Pay most descriptive for other	28.8%	65.7%	34.8%	18.7%	15.8%	7.7%
Praise is most descriptive	22.1%	17.1%	39.1%	11.0%	31.6%	15.4%
Interesting work is most descriptive	34.2%	17.1%	17.4%	58.2%	36.8%	15.4%
Organizational success is most descriptive	4.6%	0.0%	1.4%	5.5%	15.8%	7.7%
Social good is most descriptive	10.4%	0.0%	7.2%	6.6%	0.0%	53.8%

work, that individual is more likely to say that X is most descriptive of what motivates the best work of anyone, including his or her direct reports. We need better data (e.g., where we ask managers these questions and compare how different managers in the same organization answer).

The Bottom Line From the Surveys

Here is an executive summary of the takeaways from these surveys, in case reading all the details got to be too much:

- Both surveys provide one consensus result: Giving employees work that they find interesting and/or exciting is very effective or better in motivating best work. This is, according to most respondents, the proverbial motivational magic bullet. Of course, to employ this magic bullet, at a minimum you must have a good understanding about what makes work interesting and exciting to your employees. The answer to that may lie to some extent in the intrinsic motivators from the eight-category portion of the survey. And some work that must be done isn't interesting or exciting—the magic bullet can't always be employed—so we must look further.

- Beyond this, no one size fits all. When it comes to the power and impact of different motivational techniques other than interesting and/or exciting work, there is no strong consensus. Different managers are motivated differentially by the different techniques.

- Managers (probably) tend to underestimate the relative power and impact of more intrinsic and less extrinsic motivators. (This is *my* interpretation of the survey data. It is not directly implied by those data.) Employees value more things than money. To the extent that you are like my survey respondents, you probably perceive that this is true for yourself, at least to some degree, but you probably underestimate the degree to which it is true of others.

- The best answer to the question *How effective is motivational channel X or tool Y?* is, "It depends." As a practical matter, you shouldn't be looking for a universal answer but instead to understand the answer to the question *Granting that it depends, on what does it depend?* And, even more, *How effective will this or that channel/tool be in* your *specific situation?*

- With a few exceptions, the demographic characteristics captured in these surveys don't seem to have much explanatory power. The one notable exception is that people near the top of an organization—CEOs, COOs, chairs, managing partners, and so forth—are more highly motivated to take actions that are tied to the success of "their" organizations than are people further down the hierarchical chain. (When you get to prospective MBA students, success of the organization seemingly has, on average, remarkably little impact.)

NOTES

1. Mastering Employee Motivation

1 Personal communication, originally given at the Arbuckle Award Dinner, Stanford GSB, February 3, 2005.

2. Pay for Performance: The Economic Theory of Incentives

1 My sources for this story are: Edward P. Lazear, "Performance Pay and Productivity," *American Economic Review* 90 (2000), 1346–61; Brian J. Hall, Edward Lazear, and Carleen Madigan, "Performance Pay at Safelite Auto Glass (A)," Harvard Business School Case 800-291, June 2000 (Revised December 2001); and Brian J. Hall, Edward Lazear, and Carleen Madigan, "Performance Pay at Safelite Auto Glass (B)" Harvard Business School Case 800-292, June 2000 (Revised December 2001).

2 In theory, an employer who knows how risk averse is the employee, what is the employee's next best employment opportunity (which determines how much "utility" has to be left for the employee so that she doesn't quit), and who understands the statistical relationship between effort levels and observable outcomes, can implement the "optimal" incentive scheme that leaves the employer with the greatest [expected] profit, subject to keeping the employee on the job. Economics textbooks can be consulted to see how this is done. But while these formal models may help promote understanding of the basic trade-off, they are wholly impractical, and we won't bother with them here.

3 See Lazear, "Performance Pay and Productivity," op. cit.

4 For details, see Boris Groysberg, Victoria Winston, and Robin Abrahams, "Teena Lerner: Dividing the Pie at Rx Capital (Abridged)," Harvard Business School Case 409-058, November 2008 (Revised January 2012).

5 The detailed story is related in W. Earl Sasser, Jr., and Rachel Shelton, "WrapItUp: Developing a New Compensation Plan," Harvard Business School Brief Case 114-362, November 2011. The case is drawn from a real-life story, but the authors were not given permission to use the name of the restaurant chain involved, so they use fictitious names.

6 See Stephen X. Doyle, "First Federal Savings (A)," Harvard Business School Case 9-475-072, September 1975.

4. The Economics of Employment Relationships

1 You can read about the relationship between Toyota and its major subcontractors in Paul Milgrom and John Roberts, "Johnson Controls Inc.—Automotive System Group, The Georgetown, Kentucky, Plants," Stanford GSB Case BE-9, 1997.

2 Michael E Porter, *Competitive Strategy: Techniques for Analyzing Industries and Competitors* (New York: Free Press, 1980).

5. The Psychology of Employment Relationships

1 Margaret Shih, Todd L. Pittinsky, and Nalini Ambady, "Stereotype Susceptibility: Identity Salience and Shifts in Quantitative Performance," *Psychological Science* 10 (1999), 80–83.

2 Robyn A. LeBoeuf, Eldar Shafir, Julia Belyavsky Bayuk, "The conflicting choices of alternative selves," *Organizational Behavior and Human Decision Processes* 111 (2010), 48–61.

3 The HRM policies and practices of the Men's Wearhouse employ gift exchange ideas in a number of interesting ways; I heartily recommend Jeffrey Pfeffer, "The Men's Wearhouse: Success in a Declining Industry," Stanford GSB Case HR-5, 1997.

6. Psychological Theories of Motivation

1 The material in this chapter is based in large part on Kreps, "Motivating Consummate Effort," in *Evolving Approaches to the Economics of Public Policy*, ed. Jean Kimmel (Kalamazoo, MI: W. E. Upjohn Institute for Employment Research, 2016), 93–143.

2 Sources for the story of Beth Israel Hospital and primary nursing are the HBS cases Raymond A. Friedman and Caitlin Deinard, "Prepare/21 at Beth Israel Hospital (A)," Harvard Business School Case 9-491-045, 1991 and "Prepare/21 at Beth Israel Hospital (B)," Harvard Business School Case 9-491-046, 1991; Mary Koloroutis, ed., *Relationship-Based Care: A Model for Transforming Practice* (Minneapolis: Creative

Health Care Management, 2004); Ron Zemke with Dick Schaaf, *The Service Edge* (New York: New American Library, 1989); and the obituary of Joyce Clifford appearing in the *New York Times* (Paul Vitello, "Joyce Clifford, Who Pushed for 'Primary Nursing' Approach, Dies at 76," October 31, 2011, http://www.nytimes.com/2011/11/01/health/joyce-clifford-who-pushed-for-primary-nursing-approach-dies-at-76.html.

3 See Vitello, "Joyce Clifford, Who Pushed for 'Primary Nursing' Approach, Dies at 76."

4 Patricia Cohen, "A Company Copes With Backlash Against the Raise That Roared," *New York Times*, July 31, 2015, http://www.nytimes.com/2015/08/02/business/a-company-copes-with-backlash-against-the-raise-that-roared.html.

5 See Roland G. Fryer, Jr., "Financial Incentives and Student Achievement: Evidence from Randomized Trials," *Quarterly Journal of Economics* 126 (2011), 1755–98.

6 Personal communication from Roland Fryer, 2016.

7 Jody Hoffer Gittell, Julian Wimbush, and Kirstin Shu, "Beth Israel Deaconess Medical Center: Coordinating Patient Care," Harvard Business School Case 9-899-213, 2000.

8. Motivation and Your Organization

1 This list of questions draws heavily on the Five Factor framework found in Baron and Kreps, *Strategic Human Resources: Frameworks for General Managers*, New York: John Wiley & Sons, 1999. I note again my intellectual debt to Jim Baron for many of the ideas and frameworks that I use in this current book.

2 From Garth Saloner, Andrea Shepard, and Joel Podolny. *Strategic Management* (New York: Wiley, 2001).

3 See Jeffrey Pfeffer, "SAS Institute (A): A Different Approach to Incentives and People Management Practices in the Software Industry," Stanford GSB Case HR6A, 1998.

4 This scheme is adapted from David Jacobs, "Towards a Theory of Mobility and Behavior in Organizations: An Inquiry into the Consequences of Some Relationships Between Individual Performance and Organizational Success," *American Journal of Sociology*, Vol. 87 (1981), 684–707.

5 Source: Charles Euchner (under the supervision of James N. Baron), "Herman Miller: Preserving and Leveraging Culture in a Strategic Shift," Yale School of Management Case 12-019, 2014.

Appendix. The Wisdom of Crowds: What Do Managers Believe?

1 The basic structure of this part of the survey is taken from Chip Heath, "Lay Theories of Motivation Overemphasize Extrinsic Incentives," *Organizational Behavior and Human Decision Processes* 78 (1999), 25–62, but with the following difference: Heath asks his subjects to rank order the eight, from most impact to least. I ask instead for a cardinal measure of how much impact each has.

INDEX